In his new book—"Action vs. Reaction"—Gene Gorman has truly provided a business model for success for any small business owner.

Gene chronicles his life in sales from an early age—starting with selling Christmas cards door to door. What followed was a series of odd jobs—lawn cutting, a paper route, and magazine sales—all which proved to be highly successful. "Remember," he says–"success breeds success."

Coming from —as he calls it—"a financially challenged environment," Gene was able to not only "make a few bucks for myself," but began paying room and board to his parents in order to keep his family stable.

After graduating from high school, Gene served in the jungles of Vietnam as a young Sergeant in the US Marines. After completing his service time Gene returned home and led a very colorful life—which—by his own words—meant he spent much of his time staying drunk and acting crazy.

One of his first automotive sales jobs was working with a cast of characters—Docky Wocky, Fast Louie, Flaky Jake, and Ribs No Fibs—all very characteristic of the typical used cars salesmen at that time. Interestingly, Gene earned the nickname "Clean Gene" as he was very naïve about how they operated, but he did learn a lot about how he should do things right.

Fortunately, with the help of some good people, he settled down and started a career doing the only thing he had ever done—selling. Soon he became the top sales person for one of the largest new car dealers in the country for thirty straight months.

During this time he began to develop some very sound business principles which included:

- The fact is good systems and common sense approaches to success work in every business arena.
- A basic Law of the Universe says "concentrate on effort and not on results." When you do the results will come.

- When you do good things good things happen and when you do bad things, bad things happen. So just focus on doing good things and watch what happens.
- Show up where you are supposed to be, when you're supposed to be there and do the best you can. (Almost sounds like Yogi Berra.)

Soon he developed his "Winning Edge" sales program which was brilliant in its simplicity and effectiveness. The use of his "Winning Edge" sales program in his own dealerships, Gene has consistently been the number one independent automobile dealer in his highly competitive county and throughout most of south Florida every month for twenty straight years.

When some individual followed the steps in the program his sales output grew exponentially. This program also included his "Ten Steps to Success"—a simple but very effective system to follow from greeting the customer to closing out the sale and the customer follow up after the sale. His "Action vs. Reaction Selling and Management" section is a must read for all business owners and operators.

Gene summarizes his philosophy when he states "It seemed to me that if you're willing to pray, work hard and no matter what, head towards what seems to be the next right thing to do, somehow you can find a Pony in what looks like a pile of horse manure."

So sit back and enjoy the ride as you read "Action vs. Reaction."

Written by Bob Peterson, Ph.D.
Professor Emeritus, Kent State University

# Action
## versus
# Reaction
# Management

## The Key to Success in Business

## Gene Gorman

ARCHWAY
PUBLISHING

Archway Publishing books may be ordered through booksellers or by contacting:

Archway Publishing
1663 Liberty Drive
Bloomington, IN 47403
www.archwaypublishing.com
1 (888) 242-5904

Because of the dynamic nature of the Internet, any web addresses or links contained in this book may have changed since publication and may no longer be valid. The views expressed in this work are solely those of the author and do not necessarily reflect the views of the publisher, and the publisher hereby disclaims any responsibility for them.

Any people depicted in stock imagery provided by Thinkstock are models, and such images are being used for illustrative purposes only. Certain stock imagery © Thinkstock.

ISBN: 978-1-4808-4634-0 (sc)
ISBN: 978-1-4808-4633-3 (hc)
ISBN: 978-1-4808-4635-7 (e)

Library of Congress Control Number: 2017908094

Print information available on the last page.

Archway Publishing rev. date: 05/22/2017

# Contents

# Preface

I f I could have condensed this book into five chapters or even five pages, I would have done so. Over the years, I have written numerous training manuals as well as my 2014 published memoir *You Had to Be There*, and I learned early on in my career that most things that are successful are concise, precise, and simple—but above all, honest. Consequently I have written a book that is based on personal, real-life experiences, including achieving national recognition as one of the leading business consultants as well as small business owners in the United States. Presently, Gene Gorman and Associates Inc. includes my business consulting company, The Winning Edge; three independent automobile dealerships; two service centers; a warranty company; and a financial corporation. In fact, as of this writing, we have been the number-one independent automobile dealer in our highly competitive county and throughout most of South Florida every month for twenty straight years.

More important, I will be sharing how it all came about, as well as the exact same ideas I have taught thousands of salespeople, managers, and business leaders all over the United States, helping them achieve success beyond their most optimistic expectations. This includes new- and used-car dealers, as well as some of the largest corporations in America. AT&T retained me as a marketing consultant when the phone industry became competitive and they had to learn to sell phone systems. Ironically they turned to a car salesman to teach their marketing people. The list includes General Motors, as I was called upon to help reignite sales during a sluggish economy, and Cox Broadcasting, who retained me to develop their marketing plan and test-market new programming, such as HBO, Showtime, and Cinemax, to name a few. I was then called upon to teach new marketing directors how to spread the cable television industry nationwide. Real-life, commonsense approaches to success work in every business arena.

Most recently, I'm asked, "How is it you are so successful at getting this generation of sales and management people motivated to achieve such good results?"

My response is always the same. "Today's generation of employees and businesspeople are the most talented, best educated, and healthiest we have ever had … All they are looking for is a leader who can teach them the basic systems of success and hold them accountable in a positive way. People will follow leaders as long as they think the leader knows where he or she is going, so it all really starts with the leaders. Either they don't know where they are going, don't know how to get where they want to go, or, more sadly, don't take the action to go once they know where they are going." That's what this book is all about—giving today's leaders all the ammunition they need to develop a plan of confidence and inspiration to lead any team to unimaginable success.

# Acknowledgments

There are too many folks who have helped me along the way with this book to list them all. They know who they are and know I am grateful for their ideas and assistance. There are certainly a few I could not have done without—my father, Gene Gorman Sr., who taught me the fundamentals of hard work and commonsense thinking, to whom this book is dedicated; my wife, Dianne, always there to encourage me to feel free to hide out and finish my work; and my son, Owen, who runs our entire corporation, allowing me time to put the finishing touches on my manuscript. But perhaps the most important of all are the thousands of business owners, corporate officers, and sales and management people who have given me the honor of teaching them over these years. They have collectively taught me far more than I could have ever learned on my own. They have all made me a better teacher and leader, and for that, I am extremely grateful. They are the ones who motivated this book in hopes that the collective ideas contained in *Action versus Reaction Management* will find their way to the hearts and minds of the next generation of success stories.

# Introduction

I n 2014, after publishing my book *You Had to Be There*, a memoir of a miraculous life, I was approached by many of my past clients, readers, and peers, asking why I didn't put my business success ideas into book form. In addition, my publisher was, understandably, anxious for me to send them something new since they know writers have to keep writing once they get started. Momentum is important, even in writing a new book. I felt there might be some historical value in writing about the adventures of a real-life used-car dealer and the challenges faced "back in the day," as they say. Sort of a historical artifact about the automobile business since it has and continues to play such a large role in our society. I then realized, as I traveled around the nation, teaching sales and management to some of the country's largest new-car dealers, that these same ideas work in every industry. Most important, of course, is the message has to be helpful, honest, and humorous in order to hold the interest of business types, who sometimes have attention-span challenges. I think I have pulled that off.

On a more personal note, as our corporation was enjoying success beyond my wildest imagination, there was always part of my psyche that suggested a need for a good book on how to start and successfully run a small business. By this time, we had a booming consulting business, three used-car operations, two service centers, and a warranty company. In addition, we had created our own finance corporation. Things were going well. Little did I know that I would be called upon to share my ideas with some of the largest corporations in America, soon discovering that sound business concepts work in every business.

I owe the automobile business a lot, for it has provided our family with a luxurious lifestyle, educated our children, and allowed us to travel all over this great country. As you will see, all of this has taken place after I started from scratch, with nothing more than the desire to succeed. That's what this book is all about. The key, of course, for any business success story is it has to be written by someone who has been successful in business—not just successful at writing about it (sort of like the title of my first book, *You Had to Be There*).

Based on my own personal experience and after working with many highly successful folks in business, I noticed the *extremely* successful ones seem to have a need to teach and pass on what they know. I have personally found it helps me to stay somewhat *right-sized* and in some sort of ego balance. As you read the real-life story of some of my personal adventures in the automobile industry, I hope you will be entertained as well as inspired, but most important, I hope you will be energized to apply what you learn. In this book, I will be sharing all of my sales and management strategies, including how to implement your own Action versus Reaction Management plan, as well as my personal Action versus Reaction Selling system. In addition, you will be introduced to the Ten Steps to Success selling system and the nationally acclaimed Winning Edge prospecting and follow-up system.

# Chapter 1

## My First Sales Team—A Rude Awakening in the Business World

After returning from the jungles of Vietnam, as a young sergeant in the US Marines and spending the first few years home, staying drunk and crazy, I then settled down, and with the help of some good people, I started a serious career in sales. It didn't take long for me to become the top salesperson for one of the largest new-car dealers in the country, leading to numerous awards as well as national recognition. I was then offered a new-car sales manager position.

After my experience in combat as a squad leader and platoon guide, I was excited to get back into a leadership role. I also assumed my *team* would be excited to follow the program I had designed to achieve my own success. I had given a name to my personal selling system after observing my peers, who seemed to just hang out waiting for something to happen. I called it "Action versus Reaction Selling." Armed with my new excitement, I was anxious to build a team that would carry them all to a new level of success. I guess you could say I was *pumped up*.

It didn't take long for me to realize the success of most of my sales staff seemed to be more important to me than it was to them. I knew there were always going to be the top achievers, who were going to be successful regardless of who the leader was, but the average or below-average people would surely want my message of success. The rude awakening I experienced after becoming a manager gave me a personal challenge. The fact was, some of them had come to believe "average" was the best they could do. It was then that I knew I would have to come up with a plan on how to get them to rise to a new level of success. But first let's diagnose the problem.

## Comfort Zones and How to Get Out of Them

There is a long-held theory called the 80/20 rule that suggests that 80 percent of the sales in a product sales business are produced by 20 percent of the salespeople. After first hearing that assessment, I decided to do my own study as it related to automobile sales. In most cases, I found it to be pretty accurate. The next question I needed to answer was why is that the case?

While traveling the country teaching salespeople and managers from all kinds of different industries and looking at their production numbers, it became obvious the 80/20 rule is somewhat accurate in other fields as well. Could it be that 80 percent of the people in the world are, by their nature, follower-type people and 20 percent are leaders? With everything being relative, I surmised that would mean 80 percent of the athletes, doctors, and lawyers would be followers in their respective fields and 20 percent would be leaders—sort of like a wolf pack where there is an alpha wolf and the rest take on a tail-drooping, subordinate role in the pack.

Of course, that didn't sit well with me, since my role was to take all of my clients' sales teams to a higher level than they presently were achieving. Based on numbers, it became obvious that talented salespeople, as well as managers, were doing far less than they had the talent to do. Why? I like to refer to it as their personal *comfort zone*. In other words, whether they were salespeople or managers, they were doing all they needed to do to be comfortable. The question then became how do I get them out of their comfort zone and do it in a positive way? But first I had to figure out the difference between leaders and followers.

As I interviewed numerous top as well as average achievers, it was apparent the leaders all had more of one particular quality—intensity. Then I had to ask, "What breeds this intensity?" I came up with two key differences between the leaders and followers. Number 1 was need. In other words, a salesperson with a spouse, home, and two kids will generally be more intense than a salesperson who lives at home with his or her parents or has income from a different source other than his or her present job. Number 2—and perhaps the most powerful of all breeders of intensity—is ego. Ego, in business and particularly as it pertains to a salesperson, basically means how people see themselves as they relate to the rest of the team. Consequently, leaders will somehow develop a personal system of success to satisfy their need and ego and keep them at the top of the success ladder. These folks will probably be successful wherever they are and generally make up the bulk of the 20 percent leader types. So how can we get the entire team out of their comfort zone and take the team to a higher level of success? That was my challenge. I created the Action versus Reaction Management system to generate intensity to take the entire team to a new level of success.

One thing was certain, discipline and systems of control are going to be imperative for any business to succeed, but this isn't the US Marines, so the systems you put into place have to take into account the challenges of motivating people to rise to their full potential when they have the option of walking out. The truth is you can't force people to do anything they don't want to do, so the challenge becomes figuring out how to inspire and motivate them to *want* to be successful. That is a large part of what this book is all about. I discovered over the years that the will to win is more important than the skill to win. In addition, as I have preached to anyone who would listen, the battlefields of success are littered with the carcasses of talented yet unmotivated people.

Since most of my business dealings have been in the automobile business, I will naturally be using examples related to that industry. I can assure you, however, that all of the principles I teach are applicable to any type of business that requires strong leadership.

# Chapter 2

## A Little Personal History— My First General Manager's Job, The Tom Riddle Story

"**I** don't know where I'm going, but I'm making good time." After I talked my way into my first general manager job, it was obvious to me I would have to come up with a different strategy to take this dealership to a higher level of success than the previous manager, who had been fired. Since he was the previous and only guidepost this dealer had, I surmised if I was to follow his plan and was better at doing it the way he did, I might just get fired quicker. So a new strategy was in order.

Tom Riddle, the dealer, was a busy man with a number of dealerships, but I figured being a top sales producer with a little bit of leadership experience allowed me the right to lobby for the job. My presentation to get the position was strong enough to get him to say, "You got the job. In fact, I want you to take over managing both dealerships in this area."

I seemed to be able to sell anybody, including him. Now I would have to start walking the walk. Suddenly a little panic crept in.

Then an idea popped into my head. My strategy would be to pick his brain as to what his ideas and priorities were and what he felt like a good general manager should be doing to reach the company goals. Actually, I was trying to find out what I was supposed to be doing since I really didn't know. I thought I was being shrewd. I remember the conversation well. "So tell me, Tom, other than the need to increase production and customer satisfaction, what do you feel are the most important things that you want me doing to improve the company?"

He looked me dead in the eye, chuckled, and said, "You don't know what the hell you're doing, do you?" The secret was out. He then said, "You'll figure it out, I hope. You start Monday," and walked out of the room.

Hmm, this was Tuesday; I had six days to come up with a plan. Wow, six days to go from talking the talk to walking the walk.

The next morning found me at home, drinking a cup of coffee and pondering my new challenge. Confidence was not an issue—experience and knowledge were. *What made me think I could do this? Just because I was a hot-shot salesman doesn't mean I can lead a team of twenty to thirty salespeople.* Perhaps I was one of those guys who had more bullsh*t than bull. Self-doubt was creeping in again.

I had learned long ago from Jack Horner, one of my early mentors, to slow down before I got started each day, perhaps reading a few excerpts from a daily reflection or meditation book, and to take some time to think about the day ahead. Jack had been introduced to me by a friend who knew I was trying to come up with a success plan for businesses. He was a giant of a man, seventy years old, about six feet four inches, and about 250 pounds. He was totally bald with no teeth—at least he never had them in his mouth—and legally blind, so when he talked, people seemed to listen. He suggested that I find a quiet place at home and sit down alone each morning for about fifteen or twenty minutes before heading out into the rush of the day.

Once seated, I was to try to be still and think about what my goals would be for that day and how I was going to achieve them. When I first attempted to do this, all kinds of bizarre thoughts would come into my head, and it was very difficult to keep focused on my plans for the day. I had never been one of those meditation types. My strength was enthusiasm and high energy. This was all new to me, but, what the heck, why not give it a try?

When I closed my eyes, my mind often wandered back to my early days as a young boy and the lessons I learned—the hard way most of the time. Perhaps I could draw on this experience and put together a program or system to lead this team. My mind continued to drift … I thought of growing up. I thought of my dad and mom. I thought of the US Marines and Vietnam. I continued to drift. How did I get into this business stuff anyway? I wanted to be a baseball player.

I reflected back to how I had set things up for myself to become a top producer and win all those fancy sales awards. Then I settled into a strange sort of *trance* and kept drifting back and back and back …

# Chapter 3

## The Trance Theory

**Trance Day 1**

*Eight Years Old—My First Sales Job*

I grew up in a lower-income neighborhood with a mother who didn't work, not unusual in those days, and a father who was an enlisted man in the navy and gone most of the time. In addition, we had six children so there wasn't ever any extra money. Throughout those early years, all of us kids were used to putting cardboard in the bottom of our worn-out shoes, and peanut-butter-and-mayonnaise sandwiches were a pretty steady school lunch, but my parents were doing the best they could.

In spite of ours being a bit of an impoverished household, a major occurrence happened when I was a young boy that played a large role in my confidence growing up. My dad had bought the family a set of encyclopedias from a door-to-door salesman and along with it a set of books about twenty-four famous American men and women when they were young. They were written in an easy-to-read format for us preteens. The set included the youthful biographies of people like George Washington, Abe Lincoln, Clara Barton, Thomas Jefferson, Harriett Beecher Stowe, George Washington Carver, and so on. Even though the homework often wasn't getting done, I would sit in my room and devour these books. There was no color TV, cell phone, or

Internet in those days, and it was probably fortunate for me. Looking back, I see that as a pivotal period in my life. I gained tremendous confidence by reading their stories, and in spite of the circumstances at home, I thought, *If they can do it, so can I.*

When I was eight years old, in an effort to do the right thing, Mom had steered me toward a group of Cub Scouts, thinking they might afford me a little stability and companionship. Most of the guys had uniforms and all the other Cub Scout stuff. In fact, one of the guys looked like General Patton with a sash running up his side with all kinds of merit badges and medals. I remember feeling a little envious, but I knew I wouldn't be getting any Cub Scout uniform. I had already learned that was the way it was when you didn't have any money.

As fate would have it, one of the Scouts subscribed to a magazine titled *Boys' Life*, and I would read it whenever I visited him. The stories were great, but what caught my eye were the advertisements in the back. Some company was paying money for young guys like me to sell Christmas cards door-to-door and would pay 10 percent of the selling price to the sales guy. I asked my mom to explain what 10 percent meant, and she told me that if I sold ten dollars' worth of cards, I could keep a dollar of it. For some reason, I picked up on that mathematical equation instantly. Wow ... It suddenly dawned on me that I could make some money and not have to rely on whatever we could scrape by with from the monthly check Mom got from Dad. With a wife and a bunch of kids to feed, his pay didn't go very far.

I'll never forget when my first box of cards came in. I tore open the box anxiously and was overwhelmed at this new opportunity to become a salesman. Off I went, knocking on doors and taking orders. It never crossed my mind that I should give up just because a few folks slammed the door in my face. I remember the directions said it was a numbers game and success was based on the law of averages, whatever that was. I asked what that meant, and without really knowing, Mom said, "I guess it means to just keep knocking and don't worry about the rejection." I never did. Soon I was bringing home a few bucks and was even loaning money to Mom as she waited for her check "from your father."

I went back to my friend's *Boys' Life* magazine and the search for my next job. I spotted a real cool looking ad of a young guy who was selling *Grit* on street corners, and that caught my interest. *Grit* had old news that had already been in the local papers, but it was something you could sell for a nickel, standing on the corner at stoplights as the cars were coming by. As I recall, the company kept half and you kept half. You had to be twelve or thirteen to have a regular paper route and have a bike, and I didn't qualify either way, so I kept doing this type of freestyling stuff and switched back to door-to-door magazine sales when the seasons would change. I just seemed to be driven to make a few bucks for myself and knew there was no money from any other sources. This type of youthful entrepreneurship went on for the next couple of years. Before long, we had moved to a bigger house to accommodate our growing family.

After moving into our bigger house, I had a variety of typical kid's jobs for the next few years. They included lawn cutting, a paper route, magazine sales, and of course selling my seasonal greeting cards door-to-door. Flexibility was very important to me because I was now playing sports as well as going to school. It was at this time that my dad felt I should start paying room and board and half of the money from my jobs should go to Mom for my rent. My dad only knew that we were broke and I could help. He was just trying to pay the bills and keep everyone clothed and fed. I also felt a bit motivated to help my younger sisters, who had holes in their shoes as well. It's interesting, the dynamics of growing up in a large family. You develop some very valuable survival instincts.

This type of work balance would stay with me throughout all of my school years. I cannot ever remember asking for or getting any money from my parents.

I really believe my value system was established by how I grew up. Coming from a financially challenged environment made me sensitive to others who had to overcome hard times. The famous American books made me see that most leaders had to overcome many obstacles in their young lives. I saw men and women, white and black, persevere and in spite of prejudice and ridicule, stay the course and become successful. The one common denominator they all shared was they took action to change their circumstances. Blaming someone else or whining about their circumstances was never an option. Hmm, one thing was for sure; there would be no blaming and no excuses in the Riddle organization.

## Trance Day 2

### From US Marine to Salesman—Featuring Docky Wocky, Fast Louie, and the Used-Car Boys

In 1968, I received my discharge as a sergeant in the US Marine Corps. While in Vietnam, it was obvious that in addition to the many heroic individual performances in the steamy, hot jungle clashes, the leaders were the key to the overall success in the many operations and ambushes that I was involved in. I was reminded of the old cowboys and Indians movies I watched as a boy and how it was always imperative to try to take out the chief during battle. I soon would discover why.

The decisions that had to be made in an instant in jungle warfare were usually the deciding factors between success and failure, and failure usually meant the death of many brave marines. These experiences would permanently shape my ideas about leadership.

I had recently returned home from Vietnam, and after getting out of the hospital for concussion and inner-ear injuries, I suddenly awakened to the fact I had a wife and a daughter to support.

I had gotten married to my high school sweetheart at nineteen, right before going to Vietnam. I figured there might be a good chance I would get killed since I was in the infantry. With that in mind, I thought maybe my wife would get pregnant and I could at least leave a legacy. Well, she didn't get pregnant until I got home from the war, and I didn't get killed, although it was close at times. Since the only work I had ever done was selling, I figured I would be successful if I went into some type of sales.

My dad, a Pearl Harbor survivor who had retired from the navy, was a stern, commonsense kind of guy. He had gone to work selling insurance, and before long, I got a job selling insurance as well. As fate would have it, I had started doing a bit of heavy drinking, trying my best to drown out the memories of my combat experiences as well as any other experiences I could drink at. They call it PTSD today, but in those days, folks just said, "Poor Gene, ever since he came home from Vietnam, he's been drunk and crazy." They were right. It wasn't long before my drinking increased and I started developing extreme phobia and anger problems, which made it impossible for me to stay on any kind of personal success track. I mistakenly assumed it was because I had too much freedom in the insurance business. The fact was the working was interfering with the drinking. One of them had to go. You can guess which one ... but then there was the family to support. By this time, we had a beautiful little girl. I'd need some kind of job.

I convinced myself that I yearned for the tangible product selling because not only would I have a place to show up every day but I could also do a bit of the show-and-tell type of selling. *Yeah, that's what it is. I need a place to show up where they can value my many talents.* I guess the old greeting-card days were still inside of me, so I started looking at another retail type of career. In the course of conversation, my dad suggested that if I stayed in sales, I might want to sell big-ticket items, since the basic principles of sales were the same no matter what you sold. Thinking back to my early days of selling greeting cards door-to-door, I had to agree with him. I opened the local paper and started my job search. On my first interview, I managed to get a sales job at the local Dodge dealership in Norfolk, Virginia, I was now on my way.

It was 1969, the days of big muscle cars and outlandish paint jobs, sex, drugs, and rock and roll. For me, life was more along the line of booze, drugs, and rock and roll. Free love was rampant, although my drinking was such that as free as love may have been, I was always too drunk by evening to get any benefit from it.

Selling cars seemed to come easily for me after returning from the jungles of Vietnam. It also became easy for me to go out with the guys after work, and drinking became part of the regular routine.

Understandably, my marriage suffered, and it wasn't long before I was divorced. Now, with no need to come home, I was running wide open, and my personal production, once again, started to suffer.

It was about this time that I started to blame circumstances out of my control for my failures and started changing jobs. Of course, I always had a set of excuses, such as weak managers, bad pay plans, poor advertising, bad locations, too many salespeople, blah, blah, blah. In fact, as previously mentioned, over the next five years, I worked for seven different dealerships, some of them twice.

### Docky Wocky, Fast Louie, and the Used-Car Boys

The sun seemed to explode into my eyes as the hotel-room drapes were suddenly and uncaringly jerked to the side. "Oh my God, what time is it?" I hollered out to the balcony of whatever hotel we were staying in.

"Hey, Gene, I think they're looking at your car," the tourist girl from Ohio exclaimed as she stood staring at the distant beach shoreline.

I dragged my half-naked, still-drunk body toward the sliding door, and then it hit me. "My God, I left the car on the beach last night."

After a quick glance, I offered a meek good-bye to whoever she was, grabbed my clothes, and headed toward the elevator. By the time I had gotten up and run to the beach, the tide had come in just enough to get above the tires. I finally got a surfer with a four-wheel-drive Jeep to drag it out, and once it was parked on the side of the road, I left. I called the dealership and told them where their car was and that I was quitting my job because I had a better offer and had to leave right away. Could they please come get it? I failed to mention it had been in the ocean just a few hours earlier. The better offer was quitting rather than facing the wrath of the dealer for disappearing from work the night before and perhaps destroying my demo (company car). That was my MO. I had been in the car business for five years and worked for seven different dealerships, always blaming others for my failure. If it weren't for the market conditions, lack of advertising, poor pay plan, flooding the floor with salesmen, and rotten location, I could really light it up. And every time I quit somewhere, I took the problem with me … *me.*

I finally settled in to a used-car dealership called Auto Universe. It was owned by a guy with two first names, Fred Frank. I thought that a little strange, but it was a job, and now there was a child-support issue I would have to solve.

The rumor was that Fred had bought a bunch of flood cars from up in Pennsylvania and dried them out to sell to young sailors and people with bad credit. That was the word on the street. The sales staff of six was made up of a cast of characters who epitomized the vision of used-car salesmen of the day.

Nicknames were supposed to be catchy and easy for the customers to remember, so all of us had our own, which were usually put on our business cards. Most of the names had been given to these guys over the years, based on some past behaviors or habits or previous career paths.

There was Docky-Wocky; he was my new hero. He had been a navy hospital corpsman and was the image of a used-car guy. He wore polyester slacks and Ban-Lon shirts with an open collar, showing off a big gold chain around his neck to match his gaudy gold bracelet— all of it set off with white Cuban-heeled shoes. He had a gruff voice from smoking big, long cigars and drinking bourbon straight out of the bottle. All of this looked a bit ridiculous because he had a huge beer belly, and because he was so overweight, he was always seemingly exhausted. Every few minutes, he seemed to take a big breath, and on his exhale, to no one in particular, he would exclaim, "Gaawd damn!" But in fairness, when he wasn't stoned, he was the best deal closer I ever met.

Fast Louie had gotten his nickname because he talked so fast and never listened to a word anyone else said, including the customers. With machine-gun speed, he constantly walked around, muttering, "I'm talkin' 'bout, talkin' 'bout; that's what I'm talkin' 'bout." He would even say this to the customers, who usually looked at him strangely, oblivious to what he was "talkin' 'bout." He didn't care. They seemed to follow him anywhere, perhaps trying to figure out what he was "talkin' 'bout." It was really all about "Come on inside and let's see what we can do."

Flaky Jake was given his nickname because he was always stoned from taking some kind of drugs and was truly as nutty as a fruitcake. He would often come out of the bathroom with a big sh*t-eating grin on his face and white, flaky stuff coming out of his nose. When questioned about it, he would respond that he had just brushed his teeth. Docky would suggest, "Gaaawd damn, Jake, you might want to keep that toothbrush out of your nose."

The real name of Ribbs No Fibbs was Ribis Fibbs. He was an accountant-type guy who had been a big-time coin collector. He sold cars with gloves on because he had used so much acid in cleaning coins that his fingers were all eaten and disfigured. It looked like he had leprosy. When he talked, people could actually understand him, and he made the deal seem like it was the most important thing that was ever going to occur in their lives.

Stanley the Dropper, as the story goes, had gotten his nickname in the penitentiary. He had been arrested numerous times for dropping transmissions out of various muscle cars and selling them to junk dealers. When he finally got sent away, some of the other cons asked him what he was in for, and when he told them, he got his nickname.

And then there was me, Clean Gene. I'm not sure why, but Fast Louie hung this nickname on me. It probably had to do with the fact that I was so naive about how they operated that they felt I was still "clean." This would soon change, and I would start fitting in.

The experience I gained by working with this cast of characters would prove to be invaluable to me over the years. In fairness, I must say they taught me how to do a lot of things right. They also taught me how not to do it. They were the original used-car types who would establish the reputation that all car salespeople have to overcome to this day. But at that time in my career, I saw it as nothing more than having one heck of a good time while making great money. As usual, when you're being unethical, this would all soon change, and I started the typical downward slide once again. I was blaming circumstances beyond my control for my problems. It never dawned on me that the problem was me.

It was only after divorce and bankruptcy and the help of a lot of good people that I realized I would never be able to achieve any success in life unless I changed my thinking and got some help with the emotional problems (later called PTSD) I was dealing with. I had a reoccurring vision of myself standing on the side of the road with a cardboard sign that read, "Can you help a veteran out?"

After pondering the program or system I would be putting in place, I knew it would be imperative that we operate honestly and ethically, and there would be no excuses for doing things outside of the system. In other words, we definitely would operate in an honest and ethical fashion and definitely not be wearing the victim hat in the Riddle organization. I would discover all of the systems developed during the Tom Riddle challenge were applicable to any business enterprise, and I would soon be teaching them to various businesses throughout the country.

## Trance Day 3

### *Little Jack Horner and Three Rights Make a Left*

In 1976, I gave up drinking and got help with my PTSD challenges. By this time, I had been dried out in various detox facilities and state hospitals and was living on the street. It was in one of these institutions that I met a wise old sage named Jack Horner, the man who taught me to slow down before I got started each day. I had to finally admit that I was one of those folks who couldn't handle their booze, social or otherwise. I gave up drinking alcohol, and I made the decision to try to do things a little differently.

I went back to a local Toyota dealership that I had worked for in the past and was fortunate enough to get a second chance. Checkered Flag was touted as the fifth-largest import dealer in the country. They were also the same dealer whose car I had abandoned at the beach, and this gave me a chance to make amends for my previous screw-up.

The dealer was a class guy, and the environment afforded

everything you could possibly need to be successful. When I made the decision to change my thinking, I decided to use many of the sales tools I had learned from the various training programs where I had previously worked. Many of my previous managers were brilliant men but lacked the ability to stay the course. That missing link was usually caused by personal problems, such as booze, drugs, relationships, or in some cases, health problems of one type or another.

Jack soon became one of my mentors, and I listened intently whenever he would spout his logical ideas about success in life as well as business. Ironically they used to call him Little Jack, in spite of the fact he was well over six feet tall and weighed about 250 pounds. As fate would have it, his wife was an extremely short gal named Annie, and of course the nursery rhyme connection was obvious. I don't know if she was an orphan or not.

### Three Rights Make a Left

Jack had been a very successful hearing-aid salesman and dealer and suggested to me that I quit worrying about results and concentrate on effort. If the effort was there, the results usually took care of themselves. He equated it to the *law of the universe*, as pertains to business. I would later also refer to it as the *law of success*. It is based on one of Newton's well-known basic laws of physics: for every action, there is an equal and opposite reaction. All major religions have some type of principle based on the universal law. In Christianity, you often hear the proverb, "As you sow, so shall you reap." Jack simplified it by saying, "When you do good things, good things happen, and when you do bad things, bad things happen. So just focus on doing good things and watch what happens."

Of course, my response was "What if I do good things and nothing or even bad things happen?"

Seemingly flustered, he followed by saying, "Eventually the good will come, perhaps not in your time frame, but it will come exactly when it is supposed to. Just start doing good things."

I wasn't quite finished with my interrogation of this weird logic, which was so unfamiliar to me. Cautiously, I finally asked what I felt was a logical question at this stage of my learning. "How will I know if I'm doing what I'm supposed to be doing for a career?"

His response was a classic, and I couldn't argue with it. "You keep doing what you think you are supposed to be doing, based on what talent you have, until you run into a wall ... then you turn right."

I immediately barked back at him, "Well, what if I was supposed to turn left?"

After pondering for a few seconds, he finally answered, "Well ... three rights make a left, and it is along all of those seemingly wrong turns that you will learn everything you need to learn before heading in the right direction."

I finally surrendered.

### Showing Up

Jack's simple theory was to show up where you are supposed to be when you're supposed to be there and do the best you can. The results would be what they were supposed to be for each individual, based on talent and effort. In addition, if I kept showing up, I would suddenly discover, within myself, all kinds of creative ways to maximize my success potential. Ideas would somehow magically come into my mind that I could put to use to be successful. The idea of not doing what I was supposed to do was no longer an option, since I had made the commitment. The hardest part was going to be continually showing up.

Now, of course, those who can't keep showing up have a variety of excuses as to why they can't, but most of them are self-imposed rationalizations, designed to keep them from reaching their full potential. Jack had stressed the need to make a commitment not only to myself but to someone else, someone who was willing to hold me accountable on those days when I didn't feel like showing up. I made a commitment to Jack that since I had this second chance, I would try his "showing up" approach and see what happened. More important, I gave him permission to hold me accountable. The only exception would be if there was a real-life emergency. He reiterated a *real-life* emergency.

I had decided, at the end of the day 3's trance, in the Riddle organization, everyone must agree to be held accountable. This would include me. Anyone who didn't want to be held accountable would have to move on and, I hoped, go work for the competition.

## Trance Day 4

### *Action versus Reaction Selling*

As I started my journey to try to become the best I could be by the principle of showing up, I found out Jack was right. I suddenly had a new motivation to become the best I could be at what I was doing. I read books written by top sales producers from various industries and attended seminars whenever possible. I quickly learned the only difference between me and these top producers was they had made the commitment and stuck to it. Now they were being unbelievably successful. I thought back to my youthful biography book reading. *If they can do it, I can do it.*

I reflected on another bit of wisdom I received from my father growing up: "If you want to know how to do something well, go talk to the superstars in whatever field you're going into and see what they are doing and how they do it. Why reinvent the wheel?" I was also surprised to find out that top producers are more than happy to share their ideas and strategies if you walk in and tell them you heard they were top producers and then ask if they would mind if you picked their brains a bit. Feeding the ego is a powerful tool if properly used. That stuck with me, and after talking to some of the top salespeople in our local area, I remember thinking to myself, *I can do this.* The only thing I had to overcome was myself. Self-talk can be a terrible thing, and there are always the average producers who are more than happy to try to hold you back.

For some reason, I once again thought back to my marine corps days. Wherever marines were stationed, when they weren't in the woods training or in a combat zone, there was always a bulletin board in the barracks or officer quarters that had a plan of the day posted. The plan would tell you where you were supposed to be, when you were supposed to be there, and what you would need to bring as well as wear. There wasn't any question as to what you were going to do that day, and there wasn't any option for excuses. In addition, there was always a full-length mirror you had to pass as you went out the door. At the top of the mirror, it read, "Are you squared away? Do you look like a US Marine?" I guess you could say we were committed.

This stuck in my mind, and I decided, rather than coming to work and hanging around shooting the breeze with the other guys as we waited for a *live one* to come onto the car lot (sometimes called an "up"), I would take some action and establish a set of things to do daily to put the law of success into motion. I would create myself a plan of the day. I would refer to it as my daily activity report, or DAR. I knew as a salesperson, I would need to contact a certain number of potential prospects each day to achieve success. Making a certain number of calls each day was a vital part of my commitment—no excuses.

### Developing the Winning Edge Follow-Up System

Jack and many of my previous managers had also stressed that it was imperative to have a prospecting and follow-up system of some sort, so I went to the local office supply store and bought a bunch of three-by-five-inch pink index cards. I chose that size because they would easily fit into my pocket. In addition, I made them pink so they would stand out in my pocket, on my desk, and on my dresser at home. Because they were pink, I called them "hot prospect" cards. In addition, I bought a three-by-five-by-twelve-inch cardboard box with divider inserts one through thirty-one, A to Z, and January to December. I bought the entire system at the office supply store for about twenty bucks.

### How to Use the System

The cards (which fit into your pocket very easily) would be used to keep track of prospects when I first greeted them on the lot, as well as customers I sold, so that I could follow up as needed for a number of good reasons, primarily to call the customers I hadn't sold in an attempt to get them to come back. Perhaps I had a car that day that I didn't have before. I may have noticed it when I walked the lot or perhaps the manager was willing to make a deal that he couldn't make the previous day. Circumstances change quickly in the car business. These prospect cards would sit in the front of the box until they either were tossed in the garbage (for customers who bought elsewhere, weren't qualified to buy, or wouldn't call me back after I left seven messages) or placed in either the one-to-thirty-one file or the A-to-Z file for customers I had sold. It was imperative that I purge the cards when the customer wouldn't call me back. I didn't want to be a burden on someone who might be a future customer, and I didn't need the negative energy when people wouldn't return my call. I could always make another card for them if they finally called me back, but chasing a rabbit you can't catch is never a good idea.

The one-to-thirty-one daily dividers made it easy to call customers back on specific days just by placing the card behind the divider for that day. This file was also used to follow up on customers I had sold three to five work days later to ensure they were happy and to thank them for their business, as well as ask for referrals. After three to five days, they have had plenty of time for their friends and relatives to see their new car and often hear them remark, "I've been thinking of getting another car myself." Perhaps a bit of jealousy but what did I care? I was there to help. When I got a referral, I put them on a pink card and they went into the front of the box. In addition, when prospects or customers were out of town until a certain time, I could put their card in the one-to-thirty-one file to call them when they got back in town. So each day, when I came to work, I would go to that day's file and to the front of the box and those were the people I'd be calling that day.

The A-to-Z file was where I put the customers' pink cards after I sold them and after I'd made my three-to-five-day thank-you/referral call. I then had a handy file I could refer to if the customers called me or if I was going to send them a piece of mail. In addition, I could always use this file to fulfill my commitment in making my daily calls. I felt like it was important to have the same pink card handy from the initial greeting. In a strange way, the customers' pink cards became them, and all of the notes I had used were readily available to trigger my memory. The truth is if they called me and said, "Hi, Gene, this is Joe Smith," the chance I would remember Joe was not good, but once I saw his pink card, I knew exactly who he was and I might even ask, "How're Sharon and the kids doing?" Joe would think I was a genius and really must have liked him and had a real interest in his family, which, of course I did, since I hoped to someday sell him, his friends, Sharon, and all the kids in the future and ... I'm just a nice guy.

The January-to-December file I used to keep prospects' or customers' pink cards on hand until a certain month when they might be returning from a trip or perhaps a cruise or duty abroad if they were military. This is also excellent in a market where people winter down south and summer up north. Just put prospects' cards in the month they are returning and move them to the front of the box when that month arrives. They have now become "hot prospects."

### Monthly Mailer: My Master Mailing List

Perhaps the most important reason for the A-to-Z file was my monthly mailer (a small four-by-seven-inch piece of direct mail to be folded and inserted into standard letter-sized envelopes). I made the decision that I was going to send out a mailer to every one of my relatives and friends who needed to know and be constantly reminded about where I worked. They would gladly send me business, but I had to remind them of where I was even though they already knew. I used my family address book and church directory to make the first list and added all of the customers I sold each month. Obviously, the list would grow monthly because I would be adding new sold customers.

## Winning Edge Follow-up system

 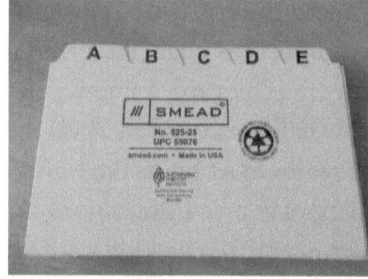

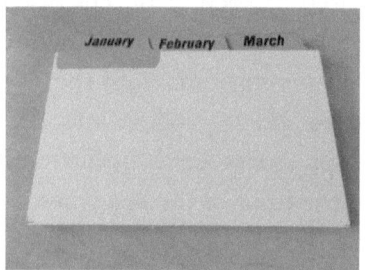 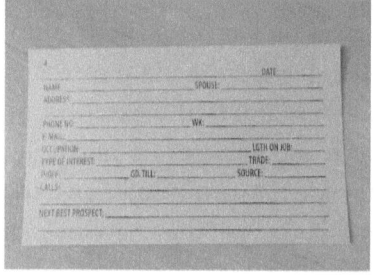

The mailer wouldn't be anything other than just a positive, upbeat message to say hello. I would choose some sort of clip art, taken out of a clip-art book provided by my printer, and it would say something like, "Please drive safely. It's back-to-school month," or "Happy Halloween. Please drive safely and watch out for the little ghosts and goblins as you drive." The clip art would feature some picture or drawing of kids playing or going to school or perhaps American flags or holiday art, depending on the season, with just a short, positive message letting my customers know I was a good guy with a good heart. It always had my picture on it, serving as a sort of personal visit from me each month. I discovered that people have a hard time throwing away something with your picture on it, so the chance of it being put somewhere that they'll see more than once is good.

In the direct-mail world, it is important to get as many *looks* as you can to get maximum effectiveness. Each month, I would have people I didn't know walk into the dealership, saying something like, "Joe sent me. Is Gene here?" Perhaps he saw Joe at the bowling alley or somewhere else, and in the course of conversation, he mentioned to Joe that he had to get a car or truck. Since Joe had gotten my mailer, he automatically thought of me and sent him over. That's the way it works. It's all about timing.

As I've already mentioned, timing is everything in sales, so everyone I knew who lived within fifty miles of the dealership and who would recognize me went on the list. In addition, after a few months, I joined the Rotary Club and added everyone on my Rotary Club roster to the list. I had joined the Rotary Club to be part of the civic world and sold cars to many of them and their employees.

I never asked for anything related to business with the mailer—people don't want you to drive them crazy—but I always put two business cards in a hand-addressed envelope with no return address on it. Since it was hand addressed with no return address, it was guaranteed to get opened. I even paid my ten-year-old son, Owen, to do the addressing for me for a while, and that was a real classic. A hand-addressed envelope, written crookedly by a child, was better than any computerized piece of direct mail, although more expensive because it required a stamp. But it was always well worth the cost. After a short time, Owen said he was "over it," and I hired a retired lady at a nursing home to do it for me. I would take her my box, church directory, and Rotary Club roster, and it would go out in the middle of each month. I chose the middle because all of the bills go out toward the end of the month, and I didn't want to be a part of that negative energy. Of course, the subtle message with two business cards speaks for itself—one for you and one for you to give away. Every six months, I would stamp a return address on the mailer just to purge in case someone had moved, but that was the only time I used a return address.

To this day, at my dealerships in Florida, in lieu of the direct-mail piece, some of my sales representatives send out a monthly calendar for people to put on their refrigerators with a magnet. Customers use this to keep track of school events or write notes about upcoming personal happenings throughout the month. This is a one-month calendar with each individual salesperson's picture on it and a brief positive message or a recipe for the month. People love it. If a salesperson leaves the company, the calendar still goes out with my and my wife's picture on it. Think about how many looks this calendar gets as people walk past or go in and out of the fridge each day. Subliminally, they anchor in their mind Gene Gorman's Auto Sales and remember when it's time to purchase or refer someone to purchase a vehicle.

Monthly Mailer Calendar

*Daily Activity Report*

I then designed myself a *daily activity report* (DAR).

The DAR was a letter-sized piece of paper that included the things I would need to do to be prepared for the day's success. I guess you could say it was my "plan of the day."

One part of my DAR was prospecting done that day. Whom should I call or text? In the beginning, I acquired a list of "orphan owners" to call. These were folks who had bought from the dealership in the past and whose salesperson was no longer with the company. In addition, I called everyone I knew who lived within fifty miles, just to let them know where I was working. This included friends, relatives, and anyone else I felt would be receptive to a call from me. I got a bit nervous about doing this and talked to Jack about it. He looked me in the eye and said, "Are you committed or not?" Prior to this, I never let anyone know because I wasn't sure I was going to be staying anywhere, but I had made the commitment.

Note—on rare occasions, when I teach salespeople around the country, new salespeople will say they have a very limited source of people to call or put on their mailing list, but when they think about everyone they know and communicate with throughout their daily lives, they can quickly make up an abundant list. Think about it. All they have to do is ask the people they interact with if they can send them some information and perhaps get their cell phone number or email address. Once you get their permission, put them on a pink card and make them part of your list. This could include people in your family address book and your parents' address book, workers at the places you shop, members of churches, people in groups or clubs or any social activities you participate in, and so on. If they would recognize you by face or name, get their phone number and address and put them on the list.

In addition, any of my salespeople who were bilingual were instructed to join associations of other folks who perhaps didn't speak English very well and put them on their list. They love to hear from salespeople who speak their language. Some of the bilingual salespeople just open the phone book and look for people with a last name that perhaps indicates they would be happy to hear from someone from the same ethnicity. No matter what language people are most comfortable with, they usually still drive.

The truth of the matter is people want to know someone to call when it's time to shop for a car. They do. They know you, or they will after you introduce yourself, but you have to remind them that you are there to help them.

### Sis Buys a Car—from Someone Else

A perfect example was my own sister. One day, I went to visit my sister for a family gathering, and in the course of the visit, she joyfully and without thinking about it said, "Hey, Bud … do you want to see my new car?"

Begrudgingly, I smiled and said, "Sure."

We then went out and looked at her new car. I assured her that she had made a good selection and got a good deal, but in the back of my mind, I said to myself, *Why didn't she come see me?* The reality was she didn't even think of me because I didn't constantly remind her of where I was. I hadn't put my relatives on my mailing list yet. I assumed they would think of me automatically. That's not how it works. They all went on my list the next day. I also put all of the mechanics and technicians in the service department on my list as well. They are excellent referral sources.

I found that if I made ten live contacts, not an easy thing to do sometimes, I seemed to kick into gear the law of success. At certain times, I made more than ten live contacts, so I had room for fifteen to twenty on my DAR, but my average to stay busy selling cars and achieve all of the pay plan bonus levels was ten. I made a commitment that unless management needed me to take an up, it was only after I had made my ten live contacts that I was free to greet customers who came on the lot.

Another side benefit of making the calls was the customers I greeted on the lot seemed to be better quality than the ones the non-prospecting salespeople would get. I was often accused of being the luckiest guy in the world. The truth is, according to Jack, my prospects were better because I deserved success. Even if the prospects I had called didn't come in, the law of the universe was working in my favor. At first, I thought he was crazy, but I soon found it to be true.

Here is an example. When I first started making the calls, I told Jack about my call commitment and assured him I wouldn't take an up until I had made my ten live contacts. As I was making the calls and facing the rejection, I noticed all the other salespeople were hanging out at the door, doing what I call the "showroom shuffle," while waiting for a customer to come on the lot—or as we say, "waiting for a live one." My fear was that all of the customers would be snatched up by these guys and I would be missing out as I was making these depressing phone calls. I started rethinking my promise to Jack. Sure enough, after the hour and a half it took me to make my calls on my first day back, all of the salespeople were either working with a customer on the lot or at their desk "working a deal," and there I was, depressed and angry at missing out. As I moped toward the door, second-guessing my commitment to Jack, a young girl came up behind me from our service department and asked if I was a salesman. Feeling a bit despondent, I told her I wasn't sure right now but I thought I was and asked how I could help her. She then informed me the guy in the service department said her car was unrepairable. She said she called her dad and he said to find out if that Toyota Corolla out front on the display island was still for sale. I told her it was. She then told me her dad said to go ahead and buy it, but it had to happen quickly because she had to drive it to college right away. Could I expedite the paperwork as quickly as possible? Within a couple of hours, her dad came up and wrote a check, and she was driving away. By this time, none of the other salespeople had closed any of their deals, and before long, they were back at the front door, hanging out empty-handed, complaining about how lucky I was. I was inclined to agree with them until I called Jack. I told him that if I hadn't gotten off the phone when I did, trying to fulfill that goofy commitment, I would have missed that girl coming out of the service department. Jack reminded me that it was only because I was on the phone that I was exactly where I was supposed to be at exactly the right moment to help that young girl as she came out of that service department. I never even looked at it that way. That example was somewhat of a life-changing experience for me. Since then, I don't question the law of success. In fact, Jack would never again inquire if I was sticking to my commitment.

### What Do I Say When I Call or Text?

In the course of becoming the best I could be with my new commitment, I purchased books, attended seminars on telemarketing, and became committed to using canned scripts and sales pitches, designed to trigger interest in what I was selling. Of course, when you are talking to people on the phone, you have to adjust to their questions or response to your pitch, but it's important to have a starting point and then get back on track as soon as you have the chance. I would always highlight the fact that we had a big promotion going on and would say, "Since it costs nothing to look, when might be a good time to for us to get together? Would afternoon or evening be best for you?" Giving choices is important when making appointments. Notice that the choices are not based on a yes-or-no question. The idea is to make an appointment where prospects will show up. Only then can you show them your product. It's sort of like when my wife would ask the kids, who didn't care much for green beans or spinach, "Do you want green beans or spinach as a vegetable tonight?" It is important to remember the 80/20 rule here. Most of the people you are talking to will be followers, looking for someone to lead them to your product. That someone is you.

Note—oftentimes, members of my present sales teams will make an appointment to send a text or email with a picture of the product their prospect may be interested in. In this day and age of busy people, this means a busy prospect and that type of technique works extremely well. But make that appointment and start that dialogue so they can go on your DAR. In this day and age, texting and emailing is very effective, and many of my salespeople take pictures or videos of the product and send them to the prospects using their phones. This is an excellent way to generate interest and push the prospects' hot buttons.

## Daily Do Doo

At the bottom of the DAR was a "Daily Do Doo" section with certain things I needed to check off before starting my day.

### SALESPERSON'S DAILY ACTIVITY REPORT

Name: _____
(* To be reviewed by manager on a daily basis)
Day/Week: _____        Date: _____
Prospecting Done Today

| # | Prospects Name | Phone | √ Source | | | Appointment Time | Results |
|---|---|---|---|---|---|---|---|
| | | | Be-Back | Referral | Cold Call | | |
| 1 | | | | | | | |
| 2 | | | | | | | |
| 3 | | | | | | | |
| 4 | | | | | | | |
| 5 | | | | | | | |
| 6 | | | | | | | |
| 7 | | | | | | | |
| 8 | | | | | | | |
| 9 | | | | | | | |
| 10 | | | | | | | |
| 11 | | | | | | | |
| 12 | | | | | | | |
| 13 | | | | | | | |
| 14 | | | | | | | |
| 15 | | | | | | | |

**Your Checklist for Success**

√ Daily Do – Doo

☐ Lot Walk Name
☐ Trade-in Look
☐ Used Inventory
☐ F & I Follow Up
☐ Smile
☐ MTD Sales
☐ Monthly Projections

**Buyers within 24 Hours – HOT BOX**

Name: _____
Phone: _____
Model: _____

Name: _____
Phone: _____
Model: _____

Name: _____
Phone: _____
Model: _____

Salesperson Daily Activity Report

## Lot Walk

Each morning, before I started making my calls or talking to potential customers on the lot, I would attach a DAR to a clipboard, go outside, and look at every car in the entire inventory. Rain or shine, there I was, making notes on pink cards about certain cars that I might have a prospect for as well as cars that I might have overlooked the previous days. Jack Horner would insist that the greater the pain, the greater the gain, so regardless of the weather, I walked that lot, sometimes with an umbrella. The average producers would look at me as if I were crazy. Perhaps they were right. My experience has shown that most people who are very successful often are considered to be a bit crazy.

### Trade-In Look

In addition, I made sure I looked at any trade-ins that may have come in the previous day. I also made it a point to talk to the manager to be sure I hadn't overlooked anything that might be hidden somewhere on the back lot or in the service department. Walking the lot ensured I would have the entire inventory fresh in my mind during the day's activities, which included talking to customers who came in or prospects I was contacting by phone throughout the day. The truth is the inventory might not have changed at all for a day or two, but it may have taken a few days for certain cars to become embedded in my memory. Regardless of change or no change, I walked the lot every day.

Note—in today's world, as mentioned earlier, contacts would include texts, emails, or other social media outlets where you can send pictures of the product you are trying to sell.

The important thing is to make the contact, which includes dialogue back and forth about selling them the product. Leaving messages doesn't count until the message is returned and dialogue is created. Cold calls are effective if you use the right script, but I have found it best to call friends, people on my master mailing list, or folks who have called or been to our place of business in the past. This might also include folks I have previously talked to about a future sale by way of social media, the website, or anywhere outside of the dealership. This helps me avoid harassing future prospects who may not want to receive calls.

*F&I Follow-Up*

After walking the lot and looking at the inventory, I would come back inside and make sure I had gotten all of the items needed from the customer to get the deal completed and funded from the bank. I knew if the dealership didn't get funded, I didn't get paid. This might include insurance information, income or pay stubs, and so on. This was listed as F&I (finance and insurance) follow-up in the daily do doo section. As previously mentioned, a copy of a DAR is included in the back of this book. Once I had started using the prospecting and follow-up system successfully, I decided to call it my Winning Edge system because it gave me a winning edge over those who didn't have a system. I decided we would all be using the Winning Edge system in the Riddle organization.

Note—Each dealership has different responsibilities for salespeople, but there are often items management needs to have the salesperson personally get from the customer to complete the deal and for it to get funded by the bank.

# Chapter 4

## The Ten Steps to Success in Selling Cars or Anything Else

The Ten Steps to Success is a systematic, nonconfrontational flow, adaptable to the successful delivery of any product or service.

The question of how to properly take a prospect through the selling process has been taught basically the same way for years. In the automobile business, there are exceptions for some dealers who have gone to a one-price-no-haggle selling system, but most dealers still do it the same old way. Whether you acquire a prospect on the Internet, via website or automotive publication, or meet him or her on the lot, at some time, it is going to boil down to a salesperson dealing with a customer face-to-face. That is, as we say, "where the rubber meets the road."

Many of the old selling systems somehow leave customers with a bad feeling about the process even when they buy a car and get the deal they want. This is the primary reason customers dislike the process of buying a car.

A few years back, I did a little study, and it showed, when considering the ten most disliked things people do in their lives, buying a car ranks second in most disliked. Going to the dentist is number one. It has always troubled me that we are ranked just behind a root canal when it comes to things people dislike doing. When I ask people why that is the case, they usually respond by saying it's because they don't do it very often and feel like they have no control. It becomes even more confusing when they try to do their research and get three or four different answers as to what a good deal should be on the vehicle they are buying or trading in. I then ask, "What would make it easier for you?"

They usually respond by saying, "If I just knew someone I could trust, it would be so much easier."

Well, with the Winning Edge follow-up system, they are going to know somebody, if at all possible, you. The reality is buying a vehicle, new or used, should be one of the most positive things they do, and it should be presented that way.

I thought back over the years at how many talented people had tried to train me with various selling systems, and many of them were excellent systems, but they usually involved steps that were uncomfortable for both the customer and the salespeople. Unfortunately most salespeople would settle into the old standby question when greeting the customer. "Howdy! Can I help ya?" This was the most common greeting used by the competition when their salespeople greeted prospects. It was often asked by a salesperson wearing sunglasses and sometimes even smoking a cigarette—not a very professional way to help people who were perhaps getting ready to make the second largest financial decision they would ever make. That was exactly how we wanted the competition to do it, but that was not how we would be doing it.

### Up System

In addition, we would not have twenty salespeople standing at the door waiting for a live one, like the competition did. This was extremely intimidating to the prospect and often would make a prospect drive right past our dealership to avoid walking the gauntlet and being on display to a lazy sales staff. We would have the next salesperson who was up at the door, and the rest of our team would be making follow-up calls or working deals. There would be an on-deck salesperson seated near the door, watching the lot and marking off the "up log" as he or she moved to the next-person-up position. In other words, we would be using an up system based on who came in first each day. We would put names on the up log as the salespeople arrived. Once the up salesperson had taken his or her up, he or she went to the bottom of the log.

Consequently, when prospects came on the lot and it was time to take them through the scary process of buying a vehicle, I took what I had learned from some of my past managers and adapted it to what I felt would make the process of buying a vehicle a professional yet joyful and nonconfrontational experience, for both the prospect and myself. The results of this were the Ten Steps to Success. I designed it for myself and decided it was the system we would be using in the Riddle organization because it worked.

## Step 1—The Greeting or Introduction

Everything started with a proper greeting when approaching prospects who had come on our lot. Keeping in mind that many of them were doing something they didn't really like to do, I knew it was imperative that we make them feel welcome. Nothing makes a prospect feel more welcome than the term *"Welcome."* So we would be greeting them with "Welcome to Riddle Honda or Acura," whatever the case may be. It was imperative salespeople weren't wearing sunglasses (prospects need to see your eyes; they already don't trust you) and that they introduce themselves with a smile, a firm handshake, and a business card right away.

In addition, it would be wise to ask for the prospect's name and phone number and put it on a pink card at the greeting for a number of commonsense reasons. First, if you don't give the prospect a business card and write his or her name down right away, both of you will forget each other's name before you even start showing him or her a car. Once you've exchanged names, you can refer to the pink card to remember whom you are talking to. The more you use each other's name, the more trust you build. Second, when you smile, people usually smile back, and that's a good way to start any relationship. Third, by asking for the prospect's name and phone number at the greeting, you assure yourself of getting what you need to follow up or call the person back if he or she doesn't buy right away. Statistics show that for new salespeople, only one out of ten are going to buy at the first greeting. It is generally a little higher for experienced salespeople and top producers because they have already been using some type of follow-up system and have a repeat and referral customer base. Those prospects usually close at a much higher percentage, but for new salespeople, it is usually one out of ten.

The good news is if you have the ability to follow up, you will usually be able to sell two or three more of those ten over the course of the next week. Based on personal experience, I surmised that prospects usually buy within forty-eight to seventy-two hours after they have started shopping. Often, when you can't make a deal, prospects leave thinking they can get a better deal somewhere else, even though they liked you. Once they start shopping and find out that they can't get a better deal, their pride may keep them from coming back in to see you. When you call those prospects back with a "Thanks for coming in yesterday" and ask what you can do to get them to come back in, you sort of give them back their dignity. Consequently, it is usually easy to get them to come back in to see you, assuming they haven't already bought. Of course, all of this is impossible if you don't have a phone number.

When first approaching prospects, you must smile, look them in the eye, and say something like "Welcome to Riddle Honda. My name is Gene Gorman, and yours? Here is one of my business cards, and before I forget, let me write your name down on this pink card, and while I'm at it, if you don't mind, could I get a daytime or cell number from you in case I need to call you back?" I always ask for the name and number in a sort of apologetic way, sort of like, "I'm terrible with names so I need to write it down, and if I don't get your number now, I'll probably forget to get it." On a rare occasion, prospects may hesitate to give you the number this early in the selling process. If that happens, just say, "No problem," and move on to the next step; however, I want the number up front if possible because if they feel like we don't have what they want or we can't make a deal, they may be hesitant to give it to me or may give me a bogus number.

Some dealerships hold a drawing every six months for a nice TV or some other gift as a motivator. This sometimes makes it more comfortable for salespeople to get the number up front, and prospects almost always give up the number and the right number at that. When they get the name, they then ask the prospects for their number so they can put their name in the box for the TV or gift drawing. That way, they can contact them when they win. This works like a charm and is a positive rather than a confrontational reason to get the prospects' information.

## Step 2—Qualifying the Prospect

In this day and age, with so much information readily available, people often already know what they are looking for. They either saw an ad or saw the product on TV or on the website or perhaps saw something as they were driving by that hit their hot button. In some instances, they aren't quite sure what they want, so you have to ask commonsense questions that will help them settle on the right vehicle. Either way, you have to get to the product and then you can start making your presentation and getting them excited. In the final analysis, getting the prospects excited is the key to closing any deal.

As previously mentioned, one of the great lessons I learned in combat in the marine corps is that people will follow you as long as you seem to know where you are going. This is also true in business. Since you have walked the lot, you know where everything is, so now you have to lead your prospects to the right product. In order to get the process started, you have to ask a few pertinent questions that will be necessary to lead them to the right vehicle.

Here are some of the logical qualifying questions you will be asking, as you casually head toward the inventory. Remember, it is important to show that you know where you are going so after the proper greeting, you immediately go to the qualifying questions.

Question 1: "So tell me, do you have any idea what you are looking for?" At this time, you will know where to lead prospects.

Question 2: "What do you know about the (for example) Honda Accord?" At this time, the prospects will tell you what they already know about the product they are interested in, and you can then highlight those hot-button features when you get to the product.

Question 3: "What will you be using your new car for?" At this time, you can focus on why this product will be perfect for this use, or you can steer them to similar products that may better fit their needs.

Question 4: "Will you be the only one involved in the selection?" At this time, you will find out if they need someone else present to make the decision. It may be necessary to let them show the vehicle to someone else. This is important to know before you start any negotiating. You certainly don't want to be negotiating on a deal that isn't the right vehicle for everyone involved.

Question 5: "What do you know about Riddle Honda?" This is the time to tell the prospects why the dealership is special, what awards it has won, and so on. In addition, you can then tell the prospects why you like working there. People like to buy from happy salespeople. In addition, it makes them feel like you might be staying there to help them with future needs, and they then have a place they can send their friends and relatives. People love to send their friends to someone they feel they can trust. They know how scary it can be to buy a car.

Question 6: "Will there be a trade involved?" This is information your manager will need to know in order to properly meet the financial needs of the prospects when it is time to make a deal.

Question 7: "Will you be paying cash or financing?" It is important to find out in a nonintimidating way the financial viability of the prospect. Unfortunately, there are some prospects who have had credit problems in the past, and if the problems are severe enough, they won't qualify for certain vehicles. It is best to know this up front in order to reassure the prospects you can overcome almost any financial challenges they may have had in the past. When you ask this question, the prospects will generally let you know if there are going to be credit challenges.

It's also important to treat all prospects with dignity, regardless of any past financial challenges. Most people have at one time or another been through some difficult economic times, and in this day and age, we can usually help them get a nice vehicle anyway. We just need to know up front, so we aren't getting prospects excited about a car that they may not be able to buy because of their credit score. We always try to get them what they want, but by asking that question, we prepare them for a possible letdown and it becomes easier to switch them if we have to.

After we have asked all of the qualifying questions, we can then establish a little rapport by asking what type of work they do and whether they have family and so on, but keep in mind, when prospects come to your dealership, they are probably busy and are there to do something that they are nervous about already. I'm reminded of Bob, from Maine. Bob was a great guy, but he had the habit of developing so much rapport with the prospects at the greeting that they just wanted to escape from him as soon as possible. He wanted to know where they were from, had they ever been to Maine, and when they told him where they were from, he felt the need to tell them about everyone he ever knew from their hometown as well as inquire as to whether they liked the Yankees or the Mets and on and on ad nauseam. Remember, the quicker you can get the selling process started, the better it is for the prospects. You can develop rapport later ... Now on to the presentation.

## Step 3—The Presentation

To make a proper presentation, it is imperative to keep the flow going smoothly and without hesitation. Remember, prospects will continue to follow as long as you lead. We use the FAB method of presentation, and we keep it simple. FAB stands for feature, advantage, and benefit. In other words, after you point out a feature of the vehicle you are showing, you mention the advantage, which leads to the benefit of that advantage. With used inventory, since you will be showing all kinds of different makes and models, you follow the same presentation method, but you just point out the obvious, using FAB.

This is what excites the prospects. For example, "Now I want you to notice one of the features of this Honda Accord is it has front-wheel drive. The advantage of front-wheel drive is easier handling and better gas mileage. The benefit to you is it will save you a lot of money over the life of the vehicle."

Another example, "Notice the sleek aerodynamic design feature of the Accord. Not only does it have the advantage of looking great, but because of that design, the benefit is it handles great and cuts through the wind easily, causing less drag, which gives you additional savings on gas."

It's really quite easy to get into the habit of using this method of presentation once you start using it. As you start your presentation, try to visualize a six-point layout of whatever vehicle you are showing. (A diagram is available in the back of this book.) Basically you start at the front of the vehicle by opening the hood and pointing out the obvious, such as the size of the engine and any other hot buttons that may be important to you. Don't get hung up on any one position. Usually three or four items at each position will suffice as long as they are presented using FAB and mentioned with enthusiasm. The key once again is to keep things moving. From under the hood, move to the driver's door (tell the prospects to take a seat) and point out three or four features on the dash, using FAB. Then have the prospects get out and open the back door. Point out items in the backseat area. Move to the trunk, open it, and point out three FAB items about this trunk. With the right prospect, I often lighten the mood by saying, "Look at this trunk; I don't think there has ever been a body in this trunk." Close the trunk and go around the other side, highlighting the design, paint, wheels, warranty, or any other hot buttons you can use to keep the enthusiasm going, always smiling as much as possible and using FAB.

There will be occasions when a prospect will ask you a question you may not know the answer to. When that happens, explain to the prospect that you don't know the answer but you'll find out in a few minutes and keep the flow going. Once again, *keep things moving.* As you get excited, the prospect will get excited. As you get to the passenger door, you then exclaim, "Now for the best part, wait until you see how this car drives. Let me go get the key." If prospects are not excited about going for a test or demo drive, they will let you know right now. They may ask you to get the key to something else they saw as you were walking around the car with them. If that's the case, get that key. Sometimes they may ask you to get a couple of keys. That's a good sign. They are excited, and that's what you have been trying to do—get them excited. This means they trust you and want to do business with you; all you have to do now is get them in the right car. Chances are excellent you will be making a deal with these prospects that day. Go get the keys.

## Step 4—The Product Demonstration

There are a number of excellent reasons you want to take the customer on a demonstration ride. The most important one is that hardly anyone is going to spend thousands of dollars to purchase a vehicle without trying it out and seeing if he or she likes the way it handles—no matter what he or she says. Sometimes, people may want to take a car to someone to show it, especially if it is a spouse who is going to be involved in the decision or a trusted mechanic if it's a used car. With management approval, we encourage prospects to show the cars to anyone they wish to. If we have done everything we were supposed to do to properly prepare the vehicle, we should never be afraid of the prospect getting a second opinion. The truth is if the prospect likes you and the dealership, you may end up selling future vehicles to people they show their cars to. In fact, their mechanic may become a referral source for other customers whose cars he works on. They may become our best advocates, and our prospects almost always come back and make the deal.

Now for some more reasons to go on a demonstration ride.
1. It builds value. On a demo ride, you have a chance to convince the prospect this will be a good investment for him or her to

make as far as a vehicle is concerned. Use affirmative questions and statements like "Isn't this what you were looking for as far as a good ride was concerned?" or "With all of these safety features, I'm sure you can see how this would be a safe vehicle for your family." Those kinds of points can best be brought up on the demo ride.

2.  The demo ride is also an excellent time to develop that additional rapport with the customer. Sometimes it can be cumbersome to sit in silence as the customer drives the vehicle, so having some personal, positive conversation is a good thing on the demo ride. You may even ask your prospects if they've ever been to Maine. Huh! Just kidding of course. In addition, it sets the prospect at ease as you prepare for the return and the key moment when you and he or she both know the magic question is about to occur. In other words, how do you get from the demo to making a deal?

3.  The demo ride is also necessary for you to really earn the right to ask for the business. In almost every case, it is advisable for the salesperson to go on the demo ride with the customer, and sometimes insurance regulations require it. There are rare occasions, however, when the customer requests to go alone. I have always felt that perhaps the prospect feels he or she needs a break from this somewhat stressful process, and the salespeople may even feel the same way. At Riddle Honda, however, unless management allowed otherwise, salespeople *would* be going on the demo ride with the prospect.

4.  There are a couple of commonsense things to consider regarding the demo ride. The salesperson should always drive first. This gives the vehicle a chance to warm up before the prospect takes the wheel. If it is cold outside, the salesperson should get the vehicle warm, and if it is hot outside, the A/C should be allowed to cool it off before the customer gets in the vehicle. Comfort is the feeling you want prospects to have when they first take the wheel. Be sure the seat is well back when the prospects get in the vehicle to show the roominess

and comfort of the vehicle. Be sure the radio station is set on an easy-listening station or off completely when the prospects get in the vehicle. On the ride itself, avoid busy traffic and less-appealing areas. You should choose a scenic route ahead of time to ensure a pleasant driving experience. Now enjoy the ride and get your courage up for the most exciting part of the entire process—the *trial close*.

## Step 5—The Trial Close

There is an old saying that nothing in business happens until somebody sells something. When I think about this, I'm awakened to the reality that, as it relates to business, there is no need for production or administrative people if there is nothing to produce or administer to. All clerical people, service people, and other support staff are dependent on somebody making a sale. This is especially true in the automobile business.

In fact, one of the most frightening moments of the selling process is when it is time to ask for the order. Nobody in his or her right mind seeks out rejection. It's sort of like crossing the dance floor as a young teen and asking that beautiful little redhead sitting with her friends for a dance. It is only when you don't fear the rejection and possible humiliation that you can make that long walk. Often, that redhead is waiting to see which one of these cowardly boys has the courage.

Prospects are like that as well. If your greeting, qualifying, presentation, and demonstration were handled properly, your prospects have comfortably been following your lead. Now, upon returning from the demonstration ride, they are usually hoping you have a gentle way of asking them to buy this vehicle that you've gotten them all excited about. It is at this key moment that most salespeople suddenly stop leading. Fear of rejection takes over, and the mood often shifts to one of stagnation. When that happens, prospects will often feel like they have to take the lead. After all, somebody's got to lead.

At this point, since the salesperson has stopped leading, prospects will often try to escape by saying, "Let me get your card," even if they really want the vehicle you have been showing them. They just aren't going to generally come out and ask, "Can I buy the car?" They are frightened as well. The exceptions to this are when prospects are leaders. When they are sold on the car, they usually will take the reins with "What's your best price?"

The truth is asking for the order can be a frightening experience. Remembering that most of the prospects (80 percent) are follower-type people being taken through the process of the sale by a follower-type salesperson, it becomes understandable. Not only is it frightening for the majority of prospects, but it is equally frightening for the majority of salespeople. So the question becomes "Why is something that should be a positive and exciting experience so frightening?" The answer is really quite simple—control. No one likes to lose control, especially when it comes to money. Since prospects don't buy cars very often, about every six or seven years for new and two to three years for used, consumers don't feel like they know what they are doing. Often, the more research they do, the more confusing it gets.

The fact is car dealers can't force people to do anything. Our job, when we close the deal, is to remind prospects of this as quickly as we can, usually upon returning from the demonstration ride. We do this with the trial close. The key to success in any selling situation and with all of the Ten Steps to Success is to control what we can control and not worry about things we can't.

The actual trial close question that works best is the one where we remind the prospects that they are going to be in control and at the same time ask for the order with a nonconfrontational question. This trial close is easy not only for the prospects to digest but also for the salesperson to ask. It is so logical that the prospects often don't even understand what you asked and you have to reassure them by repeating it.

The trial close requires us to look at a two key factors regarding the trial close question.

1.  Why do we ask it? The prospects need a leader now more than ever. There has to be a positive way to go from the

demonstration ride to getting them into the building to properly negotiate the deal.

2. When do we ask it? The best time to ask for the order by using the trial close is after you have returned from the demonstration ride. Generally as soon as you and the prospects get out of the car, they know something is about to happen. They may even have their defenses up. The salesperson should make a positive statement about the car, such as "She handles great, doesn't she?" Once the prospects answer with a positive response, the salesperson immediately but slowly asks the following question, the trial close question: "Let me ask you this ... If I can make the figures be what you want them to be on this car, can I earn your business today?"

It is such a logical question to ask that sometimes prospects are caught completely by surprise. Often they either didn't understand what you just asked or didn't hear the question properly. Anticipating something was about to happen, they may have had a ready defense on the tip of their tongue, such as "I've got one more place to look," "I've got to talk to somebody," or "Let me think about it." Regardless of their response, we assume they perhaps didn't understand the question, and they usually didn't, so we repeat the question this way: "I can appreciate that ... but if I can make the figures be what you want them to be, can I earn your business today?"

It is almost impossible to answer no to that question if your prospects are on the right car and if they have liked the way you have treated them up to this point. Sometimes they will ask, "What are you talking about, make the figures be what I want them to be?"

Your commonsense response depends on the type of prospect you are dealing with, which you found out during the qualifying questions. For example, you might say, "If I can make the price, payments, or trade-in value be what you want it to be, can I earn your business today?" What we are doing is setting the prospects' minds at ease and reminding them that they are going to be in control—because they are. When they respond with a yes, which happens about 75 percent of the time when we have gotten this far, we have them follow us inside.

History has shown in the past that most methods of getting the prospects to the closing table were somewhat evasive. The most commonly used, ineffective, and somewhat cowardly questions that are asked by the competition, which are spelled out here, fail to remind the prospects they are going to be in control. Some examples are the following:

- "Well, what do you think?"
- "So do you want to see what we can do?"
- "Do you want to talk some numbers?"

None of these questions take care of the number-one concern of most prospects—losing control.

### *80/20 Rule*

At this stage, it will be important to remember there are leader types of customers as well as follower types. My experience has shown that leader types respond very well to this question, as do followers. When dealing with leaders, it is best to let them feel like they are in total control throughout the entire process. I like to put my "humble hat" on. As long as I know where I'm going, I kind of let them lead me and respond to their ego needs as much as possible. I have also noticed leaders respect the fact that you know where you are going, based on the fact they always think they know where they're going, even when they don't.

At Riddle, there would be three steps that required memorization, and yes, there would be a test. Step 1 was the greeting, step 2 was the qualifying questions, and step 3 was the trial close question and the proper responses.

## Step 6—The Write-Up and How to Negotiate

This is the step-by-step procedure you will follow to ensure you maintain a fair gross profit when making a deal. You owe it to the prospect, the house, and the salesperson. If you have priced your inventory based on fair market value, you can expect to sell the product, either new or used, for the price posted on the window or the price advertised. It doesn't always work out that way, but ... why not? The fact is some deals will be made for more or less profit than others. A lot of factors have to be considered by the sales manager. Availability, factory incentives, and age of inventory often are considered when making a deal. I recall a prospect telling me one day during the presentation of showing him the figures, "I could have bought this same vehicle at another dealership across town for a thousand dollars less."

"Wow!" I exclaimed. "I'm surprised you didn't jump at that deal."

He then informed me that he would have if it hadn't been that purple metallic color.

"Ahh," I responded. "I know what you mean ... We almost had to give away the purple one we had. But these tan metallic ones are some of our best-selling models."

It never ceases to amaze me that the customers who seem the happiest with the deal they get are the ones who have allowed the dealer to make a fair profit. When the manager caves in to an unreasonable offer from the prospect on one of our hottest-selling products, the dealership has usually ensured an unhappy salesperson and sometimes, no matter how good the price is, an unhappy customer. The law of success seems to ensure you get what you pay for in this world, so it's important the manager is willing to say no to an unreasonable deal. It's a delicate dance to weigh age of inventory and availability of product in considering any offer the manager should be willing to take.

### So How Do You Negotiate?

Now that you have asked the trial close question and gotten a positive response, you lead the prospect into the office area. It is time to try your best to make the figures be what the prospect wants them to be. A good deal is where both parties are happy. During the write-up step, as with the other steps, it will be important to keep leading the prospect.

There is only one reason to have the prospect come inside if he or she hasn't answered yes to the trial close question. That reason would be to introduce the prospect to the sales manager before he or she leaves. This is called a TO in the car business. TO stands for turnover.

Before any prospect leaves the dealership, he or she must be introduced to the sales manager or if management is busy, a more experienced salesperson. The logic of this is twofold. 1) Sometimes the salesperson goes brain dead during the selling process and may forget about a product or a special deal, rebates, and so on that the manager knows about, or perhaps management or another salesperson can steer the process in a direction the original salesperson didn't think about. 2) Sometimes the salesperson will lose intensity and for one reason or another settle back into his or her old comfort zone. In fact, sometimes salespeople will have something going on in their personal lives that will be interrupted if they have to go through the time and process of making a sale. Knowing they have to TO everyone to the boss or another salesperson will usually keep the original salespeople on their toes and ensure that if there is a deal to be made, management will be able to find it.

Ideally the best time to TO is outside on the lot; that's where the inventory is. This means management has to be constantly on their toes to ensure a TO is readily available. At Riddle, we would strive for 100 percent TO.

Assuming the prospect has followed the salesperson inside, it is now time to try to make the figures be what the prospect wants them to be.

### Four Square

Instead of a purchase order, we would be using a "Four Square" write-up sheet to present the figures to the prospect. As with purchase orders, the Four Square has places to fill out necessary customer information as well as trade-in information. (A copy of the Four

Square is in the back of this book.) Basically, the Four Square is a deal worksheet that makes it easy for the prospect to see the only areas that come into play when considering a deal. *Remember*, before we entertain any kind of a counteroffer, the prospect deserves the chance to see what a fair deal looks like. The Four Square makes it easy for the prospect to understand. Keep in mind, prospects don't do this very often, and we do this all of the time.

The Four Square Worksheet

There are some logical and important things to consider when filling out the Four Square.

Starting at the top, fill out the Four Square completely. When prospects go through the process of answering all the questions the salesperson needs to fill out all of the information on the Four Square, they start feeling like they are buying a car, even though they haven't seen any figures yet. This takes a little time and slows things down for the first time since the greeting. Now the prospects start thinking, *Well, I'm going to have to go through this with somebody to buy a car, so since I'm already here and I like this salesperson, I might as well try to get it over with now.*

1.  Selling price—it is important to put the highest-posted selling price on the vehicle, including any additional pricing tags for new cars and the highest-posted window price for used cars. At this time, it will be important to show the discount, if there is one advertised, so the prospects can see that we are already giving them a great deal. That is all the salesperson puts on the Four Square. The other two boxes will be filled out by the sales manager.

2.  Trade information—if there is a trade-in, the salesperson needs to get the key information off the trade-in (i.e., mileage and vehicle identification number).

3.  Cash down—this square is filled out by the sales manager if the prospect wants to finance the vehicle. Of course, we found this out during the qualifying step of the ten steps. Normally, and depending on creditworthiness or credit score, a bank would like to see a 20 percent down payment. This can be satisfied by cash or equity if there is a trade. (Equity is the actual appraised value of a trade-in, minus what may be owed if there is an existing loan still on the trade-in.) Often, prospects would like to buy the vehicle with less than the 20 percent down payment. Perhaps they don't have the cash or the payoff on the trade-in is higher than the present market value of their trade-in. Depending on the prospects' credit or the bank's

willingness to make exceptions, we can sometimes make that happen, but we always show what is generally requested on the first set of figures we put in front of the prospect.

4.  Payment—the payment square is filled out by the sales manager, and it is best to offer payment ranges to give the prospects alternatives. I find it best to present a short period of time as one of the options. I also try to hold back six months when presenting payment ranges to the prospects, which I may use in the negotiating or closing of the deal step. In other words, if I know a bank will finance a particular vehicle for sixty-six months, I will present the prospect with a payment range of what the balance to be financed would be for forty-eight or sixty months, mentioning that some people like to finance for shorter periods of time than others. The truth is the shorter the finance period, the more money the prospect will save. For example, on a $20,000 car, I could say, "I've got great news, Mr. Prospect, with just $4,000 down, your payments to finance the balance would be $350 to $360 for forty-eight months or $280 to $290 for sixty. Which would work best for you?"

It's important to give options before any negotiation starts, and it gives the salesperson the opportunity to ask a nonconfrontational question.

For cash prospects, the question might be "Based on the sale price of $20,000. With 5 percent tax included, it comes to $21,000. How did you want to handle payment?" It's important to ask the question to see if there is any negotiation to be considered. Regarding new vehicles, when there is no sale price advertised, always give the prospect the chance to pay the full, fair price. Remember, it is the manufacturer's suggested retail price, or MSRP, so why not ask for what is suggested?

Now let's look at some examples of how the deal should be presented to the prospects when the salesperson gets the figures from the sales manager. This step is called *closing the sale*.

## Step 7—Closing the Sale

Now that the salesperson has the figures from the manager, it is time to present them to the prospects. That was what we agreed on with the trial close question. We asked them if we could make the figures be what they wanted them to be, if we could earn their business today, and they said yes. Now it's time to try to make the prospects want these figures. Remember, they don't do this very often, so we need to continue to lead.

It is imperative that we give the prospects choices when presenting the figures. This makes it easy for them and easy for the salesperson to keep the flow of the close going. The wording is very important and presenting the figures should be done in a positive and upbeat way. In addition, the prospects must be presented figures in a way that will allow them to feel like they are getting something that they may not be able to get unless they do the deal today. This is true for a number of reasons.

- The vehicles may not be available tomorrow. Obviously, it's one of the hottest-selling products because it's the one they want. It's easy for them to believe that if they want it, other people probably want it as well. In addition, there isn't a hotter-selling product than the one you are selling right now.
- We may be able to offer a bit of a discount if they buy today. This is true, because the dealer often pays floor-plan charges on cars in inventory on a per diem basis. Floor-plan charges are fees dealers pay to banks for the ability to use a line of credit until the vehicles they carry are sold. So you can tell prospects if they make the deal today, you may be able to get them some savings off the selling price.

It is always wise to start the negotiating right from the beginning, without giving away anything substantial that will cut into profit. Remember, prospects need to feel like they are winning. Except in rare cases, the dealer is always going to be willing to give prospects a bit of a discount, no matter how small, to make the deal today. This also gives the salesperson the ability to ask the key question: "If I could, would you ..."

### Example #1—Financing

When there is a trade-in involved, turn the Four Square around and point out the squares to the prospect. Start by moving counter-clockwise, right to left. Point out the selling price box, then the trade value, followed by cash or equity requested, and then payment options, if applicable.

"I've got great news. As you can see, the sale price is $20,000 and based on market value, the manager gave you top dollar for your trade. With just $2,000 down, your payments would be between $340 and $350 for forty-eight months or $280 and $290 for sixty months. That will include tax, licensing, and dealer fees. Which would work best for you?"

### Example #2—Cash Deal

"I've got great news, based on a selling price of $20,000, plus tax, tag, and fees, it comes to $21,500. If I can get the manager to save you an extra $100 discount for doing business today, can I earn your business?" After you have presented these options to the prospects, keep quiet until they respond.

What you have done with both of these closing questions is sought out a response from the prospects. Sometimes, because you have taken the lead and they aren't experienced at this, they may just choose a payment or say, "If you can get the manager to do this, I will buy it today." Remember, offering any discount off of an already fair price is a bargain. However, it may be that the prospects want to negotiate further. If they respond negatively to your presentation of the figures, you want to immediately start the process of bump twice and beg. What this means is if the figures in one of the boxes don't satisfy the prospects or if the $100 discount isn't enough to excite them, you may start by slowly increasing the trade value or reducing the price, cash down, or payment in small increments at least three times until they give you a yes.

### Example #3—Bump Twice and Beg

If the prospects' objection is the *selling price*, the salesperson would start the negotiating. "How about if I can get the manager to sell it to you for $19,900 or perhaps $19,800? Would that work for you?" and then "How about if I can get the manager to come down to $19,700 or $19,600, would that work?"

No matter what the prospects may say, stay in small increments. In other words, if the prospect said, "I'm not paying any more than $18,500," you would go right back with, "I don't think he can do $18,500. But if I can get him to do $19,500 or $19,400, could I earn your business?" Once you have dropped your figures the three times and in this case gotten down to $19,400, you finally would just ask, "How close to $19,400 would you be willing to go?"

It's important to keep your offer small to give credibility to your original pricing and the value of the vehicle you are trying to sell. In addition, the manager may not consider the prospect's offer to be serious if it is too low. Remember, this is obviously a high-demand vehicle.

If the objection is the trade value, you would bump twice and beg regarding the dollar amount for the trade. For example, you would say, "If I can get the boss to give you another one or two hundred dollars for your trade, can I earn your business?" and then "How about three or four hundred, would that work?" Keep moving until you get a yes.

If payments are the concern, you can bump twice and beg in $5.00 monthly increments. Keep the bump figures low. In the case of a ridiculously low payment offer from the prospect, you may end up closing the deal by taking advantage of the six months you held back from the first set of figures. Often, because of budget restrictions, payment buyers are only concerned with payments. In addition, since the prospects haven't bought a vehicle for a number of years, they may not have considered that prices have gone up, which means payments have usually gone up. We now have a way to help them without giving away the farm. In this day and age, invoice prices are often available on the Internet. This doesn't mean the dealer should sell the car for invoice. Manufacturers avail dealers certain kickback money if they sell a certain number of cars within a certain time frame, so it sometimes becomes a consideration, but if it's a hot product, the dealer should hold out until he or she can make a reasonable profit. Sometimes customers don't understand this logic, but it doesn't change the facts. The age of the unit and volume, as well as potential back-end products, such as warranty and insurance sale profits, should always be considered when taking a slim deal.

Once you have arrived at a figure prospects agree to, whether it is price, trade value, cash down, or payment, have them sign the Four Square below their offer and tell them, "Now let me take the offer to the manager." It is important to have the prospects sign the Four Square. Remember, you are trying to help the prospects get the deal they want.

### Essentials to Close

1. Always be excited when presenting the figures to the prospect.
2. Remember you are the "broker" working for the prospect.
3. Know when to be quiet. Waiting for that "yes" can be a little scary at times, so don't be impatient.
4. Be dumb like a fox. "I don't know if I can get the boss to do this, but … if I could, would you?"
5. Be a bit of an actor and have fun doing this. Remember, we are helping the prospects do something that is often scary, and they need us to make them feel at ease.

Here are a few key phrases and closing strategies that are often helpful during the negotiating stage. I like to call them the ABCs of closing the deal.

A) Ensure your deal close. When the prospect makes an offer that is somewhat ridiculous and you know it won't be accepted by management, you may have to remind the prospect that the only vehicles you sell when you aren't making any money are the cars that no one else wants. "Since we all know that you get what you pay for in this world, let me take a little more reasonable offer to management." Then go back to bumping twice and begging until you get a more reasonable offer.

B)     The "You can't get me anywhere else but here" close—sometimes it is very effective to remind the prospects that you are going to be here to help them during and after the sale. "I'm sure knowing that I'm going to be here for you after the sale is important so let me take a little more reasonable offer to the manager." Then go back to bump twice and beg until you reach a realistic offer.

C)     The "Being the top salesperson close" or "Making my bonus close"—it is always important to reiterate to the prospects that you are trying to help them get the best deal. I always like to enlighten them to the fact that "not only am I trying to get you a good deal, but selling you this vehicle will help me be top salesperson and make my bonus this month." Surprising perhaps but true, most people love to buy from the top guy and respond very well to helping the salesperson get there.

## Step 8—Delivering the Product … a Celebration

It is very important once you have arrived at a deal that the salesperson properly prepares the vehicle for delivery. This means ensuring the vehicle is spotlessly clean and the salesperson knows how to explain everything there is to know about the customer's new or used car. Remember, every car, new or used, is new to the customer.

The paperwork phase of the transaction will take place in the sales or finance manager's office. At this time, the customer will be offered the opportunity to purchase additional products, which he or she may feel are important. This will include extended warranties, as well as credit life insurance, disability insurance, and gap insurance for financed deals. These should all be offered in a nonintimidating way to ensure a continued positive experience throughout the entire transaction.

Experience has shown that often customers fear this stage of the transaction more than any other. The reason, of course, is the way it has been handled in the past. After gaining a good rapport with their salespeople, customers now often have to meet someone entirely new, and they are moved to a totally new office, which takes them out of their comfort zone. It is imperative we create future goodwill by being sensitive to this when doing the necessary paperwork and offering these products.

## Step 9—Getting Referrals Card and making a Testimonial Book

Before customers leave the dealership and usually while they are waiting to go in the F&I or sales manager's office to handle the paperwork, they will be presented with a suspect card asking for referrals. "Whom do you know, perhaps a friend, relative, or someone you work with, who one of these days might be in the market for a new or used car or truck?" This gives them something to do while waiting to take delivery and at the same time helps set up the future for the salesperson's next sale. Sometimes they will ask if they can take it home with them, and of course, that is a good sign. You will be calling them anyway in a few days to be sure they are happy, and at that time, they will have had plenty of time to show off their new car and will probably have some names for you.

BONA-FIDE CURRENT OR FUTURE SUSPECT
FOR A NEW OR USED CAR OR TRUCK

| | |
|---|---|
| Name: | Phone: |
| Address: | Possible Interest: |
| Name: | Phone: |
| Address: | Possible Interest: |
| Name: | Phone: |
| Address: | Possible Interest: |

**THE BEST SUSPECT FOR MY TRADE IS:**

Name:
Address: Phone:

Customer Name: Sales Rep:

Suspect Card

In addition, while they are waiting, the salesperson should ask if they would write a little note about how they were treated and with their permission, you would be allowed to use just their name and town as a reference for future prospects. Each salesperson has a testimonial book for future prospects to look at during the negotiating stage. This testimonial book might include military decorations and good conduct awards, as well as pictures of the salesperson's family and so on. In addition, it will include any diplomas or other types of awards the salesperson may have received during his or her adult life. Prospects like to know they are dealing with a sensitive and real-live human being when they are going through the scary process of buying a vehicle.

## Step 10—Owner Follow-Up Ad Infinitum

### What New Owners Like

New owners tell us that nothing is more important to them than a thank-you call from their salesperson after the sale. Ensure someone from the dealership calls customers within ten days to be sure they are happy and were treated right by everyone during their purchase, but this is never as important as their salesperson making that thank-you call three days after delivery. Not only does it make them feel good, but it also opens the door to asking for referrals now and in the future.

In addition, stay in touch with all of your customers on a monthly basis with a mailer that has the salesperson's picture on it. As mentioned earlier, this mailer will be a simple "hello" type of message that doesn't ask for anything related to business—perhaps a "Hope you have a great July 4" or something related to that particular month or season. This will ensure they know you are constantly thinking about them and you are still here to help them or their friends. Happy customers love to send their friends to see you, but they need to be reminded you are available to help those they send. By not staying in touch with your customers, you are almost guaranteeing they will go elsewhere to buy their next car. They don't want the embarrassment of going in to see you and finding out you don't work there anymore. That's usually what happened with their last car salesperson.

So there they are, the Ten Steps to Success. That was how we would be selling cars and trucks in the Tom Riddle organization.

## Trance Day 5

### *Action versus Reaction Management*

As I thought about what had made me so successful at selling, I decided we would be doing things my way and my first order of business with the sales team would be to see if they were on board. This might be a challenge.

### *Green Peas or Transplants*

As I went into my morning trance the day I was to start and present my plan to Tom Riddle, I was reminded of an interesting reality. It is very common for new salespeople in any industry to start off quickly and sell like crazy when they are new and then suddenly start floundering after a short period of time. Their production starts falling off, and they start looking for reasons outside of themselves as to why. It suddenly hit me and gave tremendous credence to the success of Action versus Reaction selling.

They're not sure where they're going, but they're making good time.

When green peas, or new salespeople, first join a team or company, they are usually full of enthusiasm and are very willing to follow directions or the system and do things by the book, no questions asked. This combination generally breeds success, since the book was written based on what works and they have no other guideline to follow. The law of success is working for them because it is based on doing what they know how to do. Since they are new, they don't know much usually, so they don't ask why; they just do it. Suddenly they have a bit of experience and now they are faced with the challenge of doing what they know works, and then the problems often begin. They have to overcome themselves. After basking in the glory of new-guy success, they find themselves surrounded by average producers, who are often happy to tell them all the reasons it won't last—sort of a misery-loves-company mind-set.

Transplants are the experienced guys or gals who come to your dealership from another and take off quickly, until they realize nothing is different at their new job and they have taken the original problem with them—themselves. Often, they have a lot of experience at doing it the wrong way or else they probably wouldn't have left where they were. It will only be when they overcome themselves that they will be able to rise to new levels of success.

The next concern is the salesperson who is doing a good job already and has found a way to be successful in spite of the help or lack of help he or she has been getting from management. This person has to be treated with respect, and as the old saying goes, you don't want to throw the baby out with the bathwater. It always seemed ridiculous to me to say to the top producer in a company, "You're doing a great. Now here's how I want you to start doing it." Hmm, how do I get these people on my side?

It was amazing to me that as I slowed down each morning before I got started and went into my trancelike state, the thoughts seemed to come into my head. I continuously thought about what had made me successful and how I could make that our system of success.

Implementing it would be the challenge, but I already had a strategy for that. I was finally awakened to exactly what my plan would be.

## Action versus Reaction Management Plan

### *Market Analysis—How Do the Best Do It?*

I was excited to get to work and prepared by putting all of my ideas into a type of marketing plan to present to Tom Riddle. I called it the Action versus Reaction plan, which included Action versus Reaction Selling and Action versus Reaction Management. The first order of business was to go find out how the best dealers in markets similar to ours were being successful. I told Tom Riddle about my idea to travel around the East Coast to talk to the dealers who had the best numbers and pick their brains to make sure we gave ourselves the best chance at big-time success. He seemed to like that idea and gave me the green light. I took the lead time before starting and went on my adventurous journey to visit the top dogs.

I was gratified to see almost all of the top dealers were highly organized and demanded that same organizational discipline with their managers. In addition, the dealerships were all extremely clean. It was obvious housekeeping was a high priority. No newspapers were being read in the showroom, and each sales office or cubicle was neat and clean as well.

Externally, the inventory was lined up and clean and all of the cars and trucks were merchandised in a way that the color varieties bred excitement. This indicated to me that the dealership was ordering inventory based on what was going to sell in their market area, not what the factory was trying to push. In other words, inventory was in control, a necessary requirement to keep floor-plan and other costs down and gross and net income where it should be.

Before returning, I went into the number-one dealership in the highly competitive Washington, DC, market. After picking the dealer's brain and taking notes, I was walking out through the showroom and noticed an unbelievable energy that I couldn't quite put my finger on. I paused and looked around. There were about five or six deals being worked (i.e., negotiations going on in the various cubicles with the sales force), and I noticed customers bouncing their feet to the upbeat contemporary music being played throughout the showroom. They were enjoying the music as they were buying a car. It is usually a somewhat fearful experience, but the music had them upbeat. It hit me. I couldn't wait to tell Tom Riddle we'd be putting a music system throughout the dealerships. When I got home and told him about the music, he said, "I send you all over the country, and you come back and tell me I got to put a jukebox in my dealerships?" We laughed and then ordered a music system.

After ordering the music system, I presented the prospecting and follow-up system to Tom Riddle. I explained to him that I had named our entire sales and management program Action versus Reaction Management and Action versus Reaction Selling. This would include the easy-to-use follow-up system I designed years ago for myself, the Winning Edge. The first item of discussion was to inform him we would be using cheap twenty-dollar boxes and inserts and a daily activity report (DAR) to replace the fancy computers some hot-shot sales guy had sold him a few years earlier; I suggested they obviously weren't working, or I wouldn't be the new general manager. His eyes became somewhat glazed as he thought about the thousands of dollars being replaced by cardboard, but he accepted it grudgingly. He seemed to get more excited when I told him we were going to cut the entire ad budget in half by using a monthly mailer and eliminate most of our ineffective newspaper ads. I remember him saying, "You mean we are going to put some of these ugly SOBs' pictures on a piece of mail and send it to all of our customers?" Yep!

I explained to him that we also were going to slow down turnover of salespeople with the mailer. Salespeople are less likely to just walk away when all of their friends and relatives, as well as customers, get something with their picture on it in the mail each month. And for those who did leave, we had a copy of their list so the customers could be turned over to their replacement.

As previously mentioned, in the US Marine Corps, especially in Vietnam, I learned that your troops would follow you as long as they thought you knew where you were going. We also learned the principle that "Follow me, Marines" works much better than "Go get them, you guys." Since my prospecting system, the Winning Edge, was pink cards and boxes and I knew it worked, that was what we would be using. In addition, I would be showing them the new general manager DAR that I would be using to hold myself accountable.

In those days, and even today, there are all kinds of computerized follow-up systems used by dealers. Some of them include birthday cards, cookies, cakes, flowers, and all kinds of cool stuff to go out to customers who have bought, but as mentioned earlier, the Winning Edge includes a personal monthly mailer with the salesperson's picture on it. In other words, we'd be staying in touch with owners on a monthly basis, not just on birthdays. Many of the computerized systems require owner and prospect details to be put into the computer by someone other than the salesperson who is working with the prospect, perhaps a clerk or some other type of administrative person in the dealership. The problem with that is accuracy and urgency can be lost because the hourly wage clerical person may be out sick one day or perhaps is having a bad day and doesn't enter the information correctly. Human nature being what it is, a clerk doesn't usually have the same intensity and priorities as a commission salesperson. In addition, a hot prospect is generally going to buy within forty-eight and seventy-two hours and must be contacted while still hot. In some cases, the clerk or salesperson enters the prospect information into the computer and gives a computer printout to the salesperson each day. Unfortunately, the impersonal touch of a computer printout doesn't have the same emotional connection as the pink card that was used at the initial contact point, which was made in person on the lot or by phone or website. I guess a computerized follow-up system is better than no system, but in the Riddle organization, we'd be using the Winning Edge.

### Implementing the Winning Edge Motivation Strategy

The first order of business would be a team meeting with only salespeople, establishing our Winning Edge. Then I would be meeting with each salesperson from the team I was inheriting, explaining what would be expected of them to be part of the new team. The average salesperson at Riddle was selling about eight cars per month. As usual, there were a couple of salespeople who were doing well above eight, but they were the leaders, with a healthy comfort zone. We wanted to focus on raising the average producers' numbers.

From my marketing trip, I learned the top companies were averaging ten to twelve sales per salesperson, so we had a challenge ahead of us. Based on the personal production of over twenty sales per month within a forty-eight-hour workweek, I knew what was possible if someone was committed and working the system properly. I set a realistic team goal of twelve units per salesperson after the first ninety days. I wanted us to be in that top-company world.

Based on my experience and information gathered on my marketing trip, I assumed a turnover rate of salespeople of about 10 percent per month. I figured some people wouldn't be able to accept the system disciplines or I would choose not to keep them if they didn't have the talent or couldn't fulfill their commitment. In order for us to reach three hundred cars per month, which was our goal, we would have to have thirty-three fully trained salespeople ready to go on the first day of each month. We had twenty, and because of the top producers, we were selling, ironically, two hundred units per month. We had a challenge in front of us.

### Establishing a Team's Winning Edge

The Winning Edge is the numbers of sales calculated by having all the salespeople write down on a blank piece of paper, without putting their name on it, how many sales they feel they can sell, based on their talent level, assuming management is willing to coach them in a positive way on a daily basis.

The first order of business for me in establishing any team's Winning Edge is to explain that I have their individual average monthly sales numbers in front of me. I then ask the sales team if they want to do better than they are doing now. It seems like a trick question, but it is important to get them to commit. I explain to my teams that if they do want to do better, I can help them, but if they don't, no one can help them. I then tell them their present average represents their comfort zone and the only way out of a comfort zone is to become willing to experience a little bit of discomfort. Some of the seasoned veterans get a bit nervous at this time, but they get over it. Once they all agree that they want to do better, I explain that the reason management isn't in the room is I want the sales team to feel free to respond without feeling intimidated into saying what they think they are supposed to say. The reality is I want real numbers from them and not some pie in the sky that isn't realistic.

As I gathered the Riddle team together in the meeting room at 8:00 a.m. on that first day, I handed them all a blank piece of paper and told them to write down what they felt they had the talent to sell each month. Using a blank piece of paper without their name on it freed them up to tell me the truth based on the talent they really believed they had. The Winning Edge is the average established, after having everyone pass up their sheet of paper, based on dropping the highest and lowest 10 percent to get a realistic number. I do this to keep the superstar, the salesperson who is already doing a good job of selling more than fifteen to twenty cars per month, or the sales-person who is waiting for retirement or has no ambition or talent and is somehow surviving on averaging an extremely low number of cars per month from skewing the numbers unrealistically. (There are some occasions that are exceptions, but I have found this to usually be the best way to get a true picture of what we can expect.)

In the Riddle organization, we came up with a Winning Edge of fifteen cars per month. In fact, in later years, as I was teaching car dealers around the country, the average Winning Edge was usually right around fifteen units per month, which I always found rather interesting. So in the Riddle organization, as in most of the organi-zations I have worked with in my consulting travels, the sales team knew they could do better. In this case, they knew they could do three hundred cars per month, but they were only doing two hundred.

It is at this time that I usually get the top producers on my side. I let them know that if they are already above the Winning Edge, and a few of them usually are, that they don't have to change anything they are doing, as long as it's ethical and we can properly log everyone who is coming into the dealership so we can see the success of our advertising. I have discovered that if we can change the team average upward, the top producers will automatically continue to be top producers and their production will increase because it will take more for them to be a top producer. It is by increasing the average producers' numbers that we increase everyone's numbers. Action breeds more action. So if the sales team believes they can sell three hundred units per month, but they are only selling two hundred, the question then is what seems to be the holdup? It can usually be found in management. The next meeting will be an exciting one, that's for sure—it will be with management.

## Trance Day 6

### *Meeting the Managers*

On the day of my meeting with the sales managers, which included new- and used-car managers as well as the finance mangers, it would be vital that they understood the power of the Action versus Reaction Management system we would be using. I awakened them to the fact that I was there to bring them good news. It was important to keep this new adventure positive so I was gentle but firm with my presentation.

Once they were all seated, I said, "Tom Riddle has hired me because he feels like we need to go to a new level of success and he feels like we haven't been getting the maximum potential out of the existing sales team. I assured him that it was simply a matter of a few tweaks here and there and we would become the new leaders in this highly competitive marketplace. In other words, we could catch the competition sleeping. I said, "Now is the time to implement a new way of selling and managing, and we are fortunate to have the right leadership team to implement it." They seemed to buy into it, perhaps because they didn't have a choice if they were going to stay. I just wanted to soften the blow and see if they had the talent to lead.

I continued, "One of the most powerful lessons I learned in the marines was you lead from the front and your troops will follow you as long as you seem to know where you are going. If you don't know, they may follow you for a while, but in the end, they are just going to be waiting for you to stop leading." I explained this to the managers and assured them we would not be stopping as long as I was the leader. This also meant as long as they were leaders. All we had to do was figure out where we were going.

I went on, "The good news is both Tom and I feel like the existing management team can take us where we want to go with just a few small changes." That was about as easy as I could make it. I knew most of the managers had never been trained to be managers, but that isn't unusual in the car business and perhaps in many other businesses. My first task would be to train them. That was always the part I loved.

### Introducing the Winning Edge to Management

I explained the results of the previous day's meeting with the sales team and let them know we would be hiring thirteen more salespeople to get to our goal of three hundred units per month to be leaders in our market area. Eyebrows were immediately raised, and they started looking at each other with doubt and confusion. They asked, "Where are you going to put all of these people?" and "Have you run this by Tom Riddle?" I assured them I had and he agreed with me that we could start the interviewing immediately, at the same time as we were putting in the new music system. That got a few strange glances as well. "Huh?" they exclaimed. I chuckled and told them about the plan, enlightening them on our present turnover of salespeople as well as a salesperson average of eight cars sold per month and total volume of two hundred cars sold per month. Furthermore, all salespeople below the Winning Edge would be sharing a desk with another salesperson, and we would be implementing a split-hours schedule, 9:00 to 3:00 and 3:00 to 9:00, so space wouldn't be a problem. I then explained the Winning Edge of fifteen, picked by the sales force, and how if the present sales team of twenty salespeople reached the Winning Edge, we would already be at the three hundred. However, until we got there, we were going to be adding and training salespeople. Once we had salespeople reaching the Winning Edge, we could adjust as we needed to. But the new goal of three hundred cars per month would not be an option. In other words, we wouldn't be making a touchdown eighty yards instead of one hundred yards just because we couldn't get to one hundred. I then went on to close with, "Your sales team told me they think they can get to the Winning Edge with the right training and some positive daily coaching from the sales managers ... and they are willing to be coached." I reminded them that you could only lead those who were willing to be led. Those who didn't want to be led needed to go work for the competition. The reality was that was where we wanted them to work. In fact, that was where I wanted all of the average or below-average producers working—for my competition.

### Management Daily Activity Reports

After I explained the Winning Edge and the need for salespeople below the Winning Edge to turn in a DAR each day, I told them it would be imperative for the managers to use a DAR as well. It was important for the managers to let their sales team know we were all going to be held accountable to do the things top producers, as well as top managers, did each day, reminding everybody that our goal was to be leaders in our industry and our leaders would be leading from the front not the rear.

## MGT     DAILY     DAR

**1) WALK LOT:**

Eyeball each car, looking for:

a) Lined up
b) Blue tag
c) Buyers guide
d) Open each driver door; be sure mats and interiors are clean
e) Review inventory board with inventory manager
f) Today's excitement – balloons – hoods up, red tags, etc ....

**2) INVENTORY MANAGER MEETING:**

Review what you need done for inventory to be perfect. Cars washed on assigned day – rotated Thursday p.m.

**3) AD PRICING:**

| | | |
|---|---|---|
| Fresh to 30 days | = | Blue Tag – 2000.00 |
| 30 days | = | Price at cost + 2000.00 |
| 45 days | = | Swap cars |
| 60 days | = | Price at cost + 1000.00 |
| 75 days | = | Price at cost – 500.00 ,  Swap Back |
| 90 days | = | Price at cost – 1000.00 |
| 110 days | = | Price at cost  -  2000.00 |

**4) DAILY SALES TEAM REVIEW:**

a) Review daily log each a.m. with sales people
b) Outstanding pending deals, stips, etc., what's not funded
c) Update Sales Log, Up Log, Phone Log
d) Update Sales Board
e) Update Internet & Website Sold Vehicles

**MUSTS AND NO – NO'S**

1) No delivery without all stips in and acceptable by bank
2) Note any hold checks to office
3) Never leave building without someone knowing where you are
4) Dealer requires deals go to front office ASAP with keys to trade
5) 100% T.O. – submit all deals after you have a deposit

**MGT. MEETING: Every Tuesday 8:00 A.M.**

a) Review Pricing (Bring Inventory Sheet)
b) Review Production (Bring Write Up Log)

SIGNATURE

09/01/2016

# Management DAR

## *Merchandising Strategy*

The management DAR is basically a checklist filled out daily and turned in to the general manager, ensuring the leaders don't fall back into their old ways. The management checklist will include the things that are important in the car business to ensure organization and intensity are maintained. These items will include such simple tasks as walking the lot with a clipboard in hand to make notes and with a lot attendant (an employee responsible for running errands for management and for making sure the inventory is kept in good, saleable condition). It is important that the manager puts his or her eyes on each car to make certain the inventory is well merchandised as well as clean and properly displayed, and it is imperative all necessary price and federally required warranty labels are on each car. The manager will check the appropriate box on the DAR and make note of how many ninety-day units are in inventory.

In addition, it is important to have the inventory rotated on a regular basis, with a good and varied color mix. All displayed inventory should be rotated and washed at least twice a week. Vehicles on the left should go to the right and vice versa. The sales team should be involved in this task. Activity breeds activity as well as gets the sales team excited about what they are going to be selling. In addition, the oldest inventory should be prominently arranged to ensure the oldest units are sold first if at all possible. Regarding new-car inventory, often neglect or laziness has fresh inventory sold first when there is the exact same model sitting somewhere in one of the back rows that is going to cost the dealership money as it starts aging—sort of like the bread route salesman who needs to rotate the shelf in the grocery store. In our case, the expense of having old units is much more than a loaf of bread.

### Inventory Meeting

In addition to proper merchandising, each month we would be holding a meeting showing how many of each make and model we had in stock, how many were ordered, and how many of that exact make and model we averaged selling per month. This would ensure we were only ordering what we needed and not reacting to personal or factory delusions of what might sell in the future. There's a fine line between having too many of something and too few. Except in a few rare promotional types of cases or factory delivery time concerns, if we only sell three of a certain make and model each month and six more are on the way, we don't need twenty-five in stock. My experience has shown that urgency sells, and good inventory control is a key consideration to maintaining good gross profit while keeping floor-plan costs down.

## Used-Car Pricing Strategy

Our pricing of inventory would be a big part of inventory control as well as profit potential. Except for a few new vehicles, it is common knowledge that used cars generally offer the greatest opportunity for gross profit. The fact is each used car is unique, and there is never one exactly like the one we have anywhere else. This is not true with new cars and trucks, and often advertising is so ruthless regarding price discounts, the dealer's only way of making a reasonable profit on new cars and trucks is based on selling a variety of warranty and insurance products, as well as finance, gap insurance, and reserve profits for financed deals.

Accordingly, all used cars would have retail prices on the window stickers. We would not be insulting the consumer's intelligence by leaving the prices off of the cars. In addition, the salespeople would not have to stumble around looking like idiots or trying to look the price up on a used-car list when the customers asked how much a car cost. If we bought or traded our used cars in for the right money, we would be competitive and would never be ashamed of our prices. Markups should be based on our cost, plus any additional work, warranties, or any other expenses incurred to the vehicle before it was put on the lot for sale.

In addition, we would advertise prices for used cars based on age, and all of our price ads, newspaper as well as auto publications, Internet, and web pages, would be adjusted as inventory aged. For a vehicle that was fresh, whether it came from trade-ins, auction purchases, or private owner purchases, we would use the same strategy. When a car was frontline ready, in other words, once it had been through our shop and was in pristine condition and ready to sell, it would be advertised based on market conditions for that particular vehicle but never less than the NADA retail or *Kelly Blue Book* value with all of the adds, such as mileage adjustments or various packages or equipment that were not standard for that particular vehicle. It often occurs that for one reason or other, a dealer will be able to buy a car for below market wholesale price. In those instances, the pricing of the vehicle should still be based on the aforementioned pricing strategy.

All trade-ins should be appraised for the actual worth of the traded vehicle. It will be imperative that all expenses to get the trade frontline ready be deducted from the actual value of the trade. Management should never cut the trade value to try to protect them from making a mistake. In other words, we wouldn't try to steal the trade. It was worth what it was worth, and the prospect should get what his or her trade was really worth when making the deal. This would enhance the potential profit on the vehicle the prospect was purchasing. It was important to remember we would only get one chance to make a fair profit on the vehicle we were selling.

It would be mandatory that the manager invest in the entire used-car inventory to have it look as new as possible. Most of the time, if a product didn't sell within ninety days, it was because a manager chose not to fix something trivial. Not only does that turn off the salespeople, who hate to have to explain why we didn't fix something that should have been fixed, but it turns off the customer as well, and it could have been avoided if we had just fixed it to begin with. This would include paint, dents, missing parts, tires with low tread, and so on. If the buyer or manager had traded the vehicle in properly, they would have accounted for these discrepancies, and it would not have affected the potential profit margin once sold. It is important to note that customers may come by when the dealership is closed, and if the inventory isn't in pristine condition as they browse, the chances of them coming back when it is open are very slim.

The truth was, however, that sometimes we had a vehicle that just didn't sell for some unknown reason. Perhaps the market had changed as it sometimes did or there were too many of these types of vehicles in our market area. Whatever the case, as the car aged in our inventory, we would lower the price in all of our ads, on our websites, and so on accordingly. For example, after thirty days, we would lower pricing by $1,000 below the sticker price. After forty-five days, we would lower it by $1,500, and after sixty days by $2,000. Once a car got to be seventy-five days old, we would advertise and sell it for what we felt like we could get if we took it to the auction. (Except in rare cases, all vehicles that were ninety days old would be going to the auction.) Any further negotiating would take place from the new lowered price. This would generally spur on prospects who might otherwise not have considered the car to take a look. The managers would have to check the box where they ensured they had adjusted their ads for the day per the pricing strategy. They were highly motivated because part of their compensation was based on the end-of-month gross profit, and with our policy that all ninety-day units went to the auction, the money lost on cars we had to unload was deducted from their month-end gross profit.

Often, people are anxious to just get a deal. In this day and age, people have all of the tools available to research what a deal is, and I would rather sell them our aged inventory for auction money than have to take it to an auction, where I'll have to pay fees and transportation costs. In addition, they usually say all kinds of good things about the deal they got, and we'll still have a chance to sell them a warranty and perhaps some insurance products, which often can make the dealership substantial profit.

### Inventory Control Board

Each day, the used-car manager would stand in front of the inventory control board with the lot attendant and look at the status of the used-car inventory. The inventory control board would have the entire used-car inventory listed and would be used to ensure each vehicle had been through our process. The board would have a checklist to be maintained by an assigned member of the office staff who stocked in the vehicle. After the vehicle had been stocked in, using the bill of sale from where we purchased it or a copy of the final purchase order if we traded it in, the details were then entered into the computer with retail pricing as well as cost figures with any adds for any other expenses. In addition, a jacket or folder was then made for each used vehicle. Inside this folder would be a copy of our ninety-nine-point gold check certification to ensure everything that needed to be done to make the vehicle frontline ready had been done, a copy of the detail checklist, and repair orders (ROs) for oil and fluids changed, inspections, extra key receipts, and so on. The folder would ensure all ROs were available, and the board would ensure anything that had to be ordered was ordered, and the date it was ordered or sent out to have work done would be written on the comments section of the board. A copy of each checklist or RO for the work done would be put into the jacket. The office staff member would be responsible for maintaining the board, deleting cars that were sold, and adding used-car inventory as it came in. This would allow us to put a used-car warranty on each car, giving the potential customer peace of mind, which is vital to all used-car customers. New- and used-car inventory would all be updated in the computer automatically, but the used cars had to also be on the inventory control board. By reviewing the inventory board daily with the lot attendant, the used-car manager would know when the ball was being dropped by one of the service outlets that might be working on one of the cars and keep abreast of what was going on. In other words, negligence might be the only thing keeping one of his or her vehicles off of the front line and consequently getting older. The old out of sight, out of mind theory is true in this case. The manager would check the box on the DAR, verifying he or she had reviewed the board each day.

The habit of being held accountable on a daily basis is difficult to get into. The old habits of coming to work each day and reacting to the needs and problems of the day are difficult to break and easy to do in the car business, but the fact is if you keep doing what you've been doing, you'll keep getting what you've been getting. In most instances, the areas that management reacts to each day would automatically be taken care of if the manager was doing what was on the DAR.

## Inventory Control Board

### *Daily Log Sheets*

First was the traffic log. There would be a traffic control log kept at the front of the showroom to be filled out by the salesperson, showing the name, phone number, and product shown for each prospect who came on the lot or into the dealership. In addition, there would be a place to put the name of the manager who was introduced to the prospect before he or she left if he or she didn't purchase.

Second was the phone log. There would be a phone log kept with the operator showing the name of any prospect who called the company during the day and which salesperson was given that call.

Daily Log Sheets

## Silent Motivators

The gross log was a daily gross profit record kept by management for each deal sold throughout the month. This log would show the accumulative profit from all sources, including warranties, reserve, insurances, and so on, as each sold deal was delivered. This was what we called a "silent motivator." By having to keep track of the accumulative profit and knowing what their goal and bonus target were each month, the managers automatically turned up their intensity without even realizing it.

| NAME | DATE | SALES | STOCK # | YR & MODEL | TRADE | ACV | GROSS | RES | WAR | GAP | MTD | UNIT | TRADE | GROSS | LENDER |
|---|---|---|---|---|---|---|---|---|---|---|---|---|---|---|---|
| | | | | | | | | | | | #VALUE! | | | #VALUE! | |
| | | | | | | | | | | | #VALUE! | | | $0 | |
| | | | | | | | | | | | #VALUE! | | | $0 | |
| | | | | | | | | | | | #VALUE! | | | $0 | |
| | | | | | | | | | | | #VALUE! | | | $0 | |
| | | | | | | | | | | | #VALUE! | | | $0 | |
| | | | | | | | | | | | #VALUE! | | | $0 | |
| | | | | | | | | | | | #VALUE! | | | $0 | |
| | | | | | | | | | | | #VALUE! | | | $0 | |
| | | | | | | | | | | | #VALUE! | | | $0 | |
| | | | | | | | | | | | #VALUE! | | | $0 | |
| | | | | | | | | | | | #VALUE! | | | $0 | |
| | | | | | | | | | | | #VALUE! | | | $0 | |
| | | | | | | | | | | | #VALUE! | | | $0 | |
| | | | | | | | | | | | #VALUE! | | | $0 | |
| | | | | | | | | | | | #VALUE! | | | $0 | |
| | | | | | | | | | | | #VALUE! | | | $0 | |
| | | | | | | | | | | | #VALUE! | | | $0 | |
| | | | | | | | | | | | #VALUE! | | | $0 | |
| | | | | | | | | | | | #VALUE! | | | $0 | |

GENE GORMAN PREMIER AUTO SALES
RETAIL WRITE UP LOG

Gross log

A sales board would be posted in a visible spot for all to see, showing how many sales each salesperson had delivered throughout the month. This board was to be updated each morning by the previous month's lowest-producing salesperson. Not only did this silently motivate the entire team, because everyone could see how everyone else was doing, but it generally motivated the previous month's lowest salesperson to turn the intensity up.

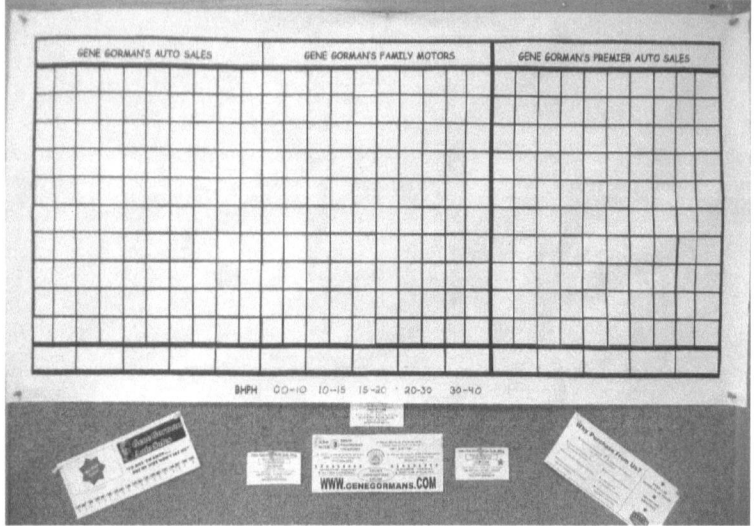

Sales Board

The sales manager would also keep an appointment board in his or her office, showing what appointments each salesperson had for that day. If the salesperson was working the system properly, he or she should have appointments and the goal should be for each salesperson to have at least two appointments a day.

Appointment Boards

My experience has shown that you have to be conditioned to be successful, just as you have to get in shape to become a long-distance runner. This is most evident when you consider that salespeople as well as managers have a habit of performing well one month and then settling into a comfort zone and dropping back to average the next month. To become a leading company, high performance has to become the new normal.

### Coaching the Sales Team

In order to be a top company and a leader in any industry, everybody needs to be coached. Top producers need a coach to help them deal with being a top producer. This includes leaving them alone as long as they are doing a good job honestly and ethically and treating them with the amount of respect that the top producers deserve. This of course then serves as an incentive for average producers to become top producers.

Average producers need coaching to help them become top producers, assuming they want to become top producers. If they don't, then we have a different kind of challenge. It's important to remember everyone has different talents as well as priorities in life and the bulk of the sales force will always be average producers. Our goal is to raise the average.

### How to Coach

It all starts with the coach's commitment to the sales team, which is required by all managers:

- As your coach, I'm going to give you a set of commonsense tools to use on a regular basis. These will be the same tools that top producers use nationwide.
- As your coach, I'm going to review these tools with you daily and help you develop the habit of using these tools daily. There will be a struggle here because the old habit of doing the things average producers do—or perhaps don't do—is more comfortable, which is why average producers are average.
- As your coach, I'm going to always try to focus on what part of the new tools the average producers are using properly and build on them. It will be important to praise any amount of progress. As someone once said, "Always try to catch your

kids or employees doing something right and praise that."
(You can't build on what they are doing wrong or not doing
at all.)

- Finally, as your coach, I'm going to stay committed to coach-
ing you daily—even when I don't want to and you don't want
me to—until you have reached the Winning Edge.
- I commit to the following commonsense tools:
  - ☐ Training—I commit, as your coach, *you will be trained*!
  - ☐ Workbook—you will be provided with an Action versus Reaction Selling workbook. This workbook will include everything you need to be successful, including the "Ten Steps to Success."

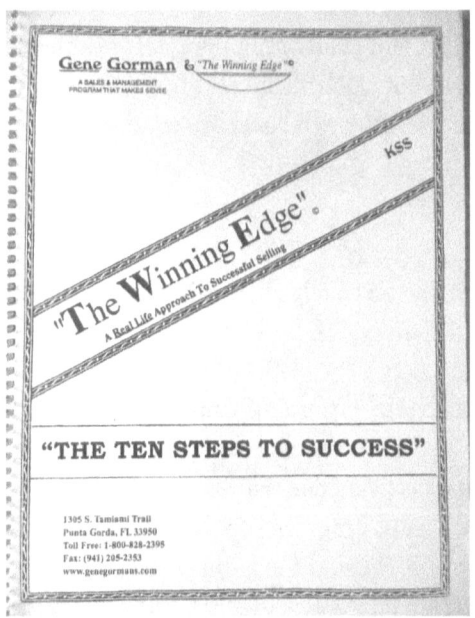

Ten Steps to Success Workbook

- ☐ Follow-up system—you will be provided with a new Winning Edge follow-up system to use during training and during your day-to-day activities.

☐ Two-phase daily coaching will be required for all salespeople below the Winning Edge level for the previous month (except for vacation months or those who are above yet want to be continually coached).

☐ Log review—each morning the sales manager will review the previous day's traffic log and phone log with the sales team. He or she will ask to see the hot prospect pink card with a daytime phone number for each prospect appearing on the logs. This will ensure the salesperson is greeting prospects properly and handling the phone prospects properly.

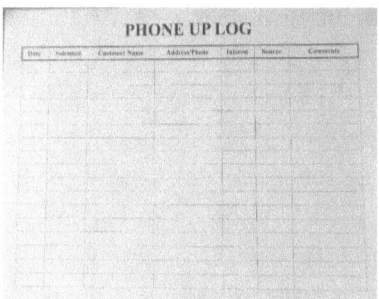

Phone log

☐ DAR review—each salesperson below the Winning Edge turns in his or her DAR showing what calls he or she has made for the previous day and what appointments he or she has for the present day. If a salesperson is making calls, using the scripts as taught in training, and using the follow-up system, he or she will be making appointments. These appointments should show up in the hot box section of their DAR and will be posted on a manager's appointment board in the sales office. History shows that over 50 percent of all appointments buy, so ideally, each salesperson should have two appointments daily.

*What's the Psychology behind All of This?*

If coaches are consistent with their daily coaching, the salespeople start figuring that since they have to show their pink cards, they might as well start greeting and handling phone ups properly. And since they have to make ten contacts per day, they might as well call the people on the pink cards. And since they have to call these people and put them on their DAR, they might as well use the scripts. That way, they can make appointments so they can have some people to put in the hot box during the following day's often intimidating daily coaching session.

*Results*

Once management has developed the habit of coaching the sales team daily, the sales team develops the habit of doing the things top producers do daily. When they start doing these things, they start reaping what they are sowing and the law of success becomes a reality.

It is important to remember the reason for failure in any system is not the lack of getting followers to become leaders; it is getting the leaders to consistently lead. Coaching your sales team will be the individual test on how committed and capable each manager is in helping the organization become a top company.

The journey in taking the Riddle team to the top was a resounding success. In just over three months, we raised the average from eight to twelve and never looked back. Not only did we raise the average, but we also raised the average gross profit by over five hundred dollars per deal. All of this was accomplished by sticking to the systems we implemented, negotiating deals from the top price down, rather than starting at the bottom, and staying positive during the accountability process. Integrity and commitment worked far better than even I had imagined. I guess Jack Horner was right.

The most exciting experience was to see the pride the entire team took in becoming an industry leader. Discipline was a key factor, and there was a bit of resistance in the beginning. After losing a few who didn't want to do better, we built a team that seemed to have some swagger.

### Service Department Challenge

One of my biggest challenges was to get the customer satisfaction index (CSI) level higher. In those days, inventory was often controlled by the factory, based on how good the CSI reports were. As the sales team was making their calls and I reviewed the CSI reports, it was apparent the service CSI was much lower than the average. I surmised that a bad service experience was going to affect the sales potential. When customers are treated badly in service, they turn against the entire operation and will go elsewhere to buy their next car. After doing a bit of investigating, I found that the two service advisers, who stood side by side, had turned the approach they had with customers into a sarcastic, often confrontational experience. They were old friends and seemed to try to impress each other with their rolling eyes and passive-aggressive mannerisms. Customers often told us they felt like they were inconveniencing the people they were doing business with, leaving them with a bad feeling when they left. Getting them back to sell them another car would be a challenge if we didn't make some changes.

The truth of the matter was the service advisers hadn't been properly trained and kept accountable by the leaders. We fixed that by making a few personnel changes and training the new advisers on how important their role was. That was all it took. Get them to commit to change and then hold them accountable in a positive way.

# Chapter 5

## Tom Riddle Becomes My Mentor

It wasn't long before Tom Riddle was getting questioned on how he had achieved this rapid turnaround. He told a few of his peers he would explain it all at the next peer group meeting in San Francisco.

The peer groups were officially referred to as "Twenty Groups." These groups were made up of approximately twenty dealers from different parts of the country that were similar in market size. About three or four times each year, they would meet at a nice location and have what might be called a working vacation. Each dealer would have a copy of the financial statements for all of the dealers in their Twenty Group. The idea was to share what was working well for some with those who might be weak in that particular area. In Tom's case, they wanted to know how in the world he got his grosses and volume up so quickly.

I'll never forget the day he walked into my office and said, "Come on; let's go for a ride."

"Where we going?" I asked.

After a few miles, we pulled up in front of an exclusive men's store called the Quality Shop. Going inside, he told the manager, "Get this guy decked out in two of your finest suits."

Little did I know he wanted to show me off to his Twenty Group, and he wanted me looking good. I was going to be the fair-haired boy and the one to explain how we had turned this thing around so quickly. I had remarried, and within a week, my wife, Dianne, and I joined him and his wife, Julia, in beautiful San Francisco.

It was a terrific trip, and on the way back, Tom mentioned that I probably was going to be asked to take a few more trips to put my Action versus Reaction plan into some of the Twenty Group members' dealerships. I assured him that I already had a pretty busy schedule. He smiled and said, "We'll talk when we get back."

After a few days, when we got back from San Francisco, Tom told me he had been getting some calls from his Twenty Group buddies, and they were putting the heat on him to let me come to their dealerships and put our program of Action versus Reaction in their operations. It was at that time he offered what was probably the most unselfish proposition I've ever encountered in business. He told me that what I had was something very special, and as much as he would hate to see me leave, he felt like it needed to be shared with the entire industry. I didn't really know what to say. Was he sincere, or was this just another way dealers sometimes eased their leader out once they knew how to make things happen? It wasn't unusual for dealers to start doubting the need for the leader who turned things around, and they sometimes started feeling that perhaps they could get it done for less. No, that wouldn't be Tom Riddle. He was sincere. In fact, there was a very powerful experience that sealed our relationship beyond the car business.

Shortly after I joined Tom, as we were starting to achieve our goals, he was suddenly faced with a family tragedy. His oldest son had just returned home to die. He had the AIDS virus. There wasn't much known about AIDS in those days, and if you got it, it was certainly a death sentence. One morning, Tom, a strong and positive man, came into work and was visibly shaken. I asked him what was wrong, and he said he was sad for his son because no one would visit him for fear of contracting the disease. I guess Raymond Johnson, a gay fellow I stood up for in school who was being bullied, ran through my mind, so I asked if he would like me to go see him. Surprisingly, he said, "Would you mind?"

I said, "I would be happy to go." I had never been close to someone with AIDS, but my faith was strong and I just felt the need to do it.

The next morning, on my way in to work, I stopped and met his son. He was very frail and could barely speak. He had a wet cloth on his head, and Tom's wife, Julia, was in the room. I told him how much his dad meant to me and how he told everyone at work he loved him. Then I said I wanted to come see him because I knew he was special. I asked him if he had faith in the next life, and he said he did. I touched his arm and said I hoped to see him in the next life someday. I then left and tried not to question myself about why I had gone to see him. All I knew was it felt good and felt right.

No, Tom Riddle was sincere about wanting me to carry my message to other businesses. In addition, he insisted that I keep him on the client list and continue to work with his company on a quarterly basis. Of course I said yes.

Armed with his Twenty Group list and a few already scheduled clients, whom I had met in San Francisco, and after getting the approval and "Go get 'em, tiger" from Dianne, I was on my way. In 1986, I formed my company Gene Gorman and Associates Inc.

Tom Riddle, who passed in 2005, was one of the most positive men I've ever been around. He was to become a good friend and as such was the real life example of the exact procedures used at all of the dealerships I taught, consulted, and trained around the country. Considering Tom brought me on board to take his dealerships to a higher level of success, which we did, and then encouraged me to take my message all over the country, it goes without saying that his unselfish vision taught me more than I ever taught him.

# Chapter 6

## Gene Gorman and Associates Inc.

### Teaching Action versus Reaction Management around the Good Old USA

The next few months kept me busy, flying all over the place and introducing the Action versus Reaction program to dealers on Tom's Twenty Group list. Many of these dealers were also megadealers, dealers who have more than one product line, and many of them belonged to numerous Twenty Groups.

Before long, I was booking myself all over the United States, including Hawaii and Alaska. I had been hired by General Motors to train their dealers in various parts of the country, and by way of my Rotary Club membership, I was asked to help AT&T with some of their marketing and motivational needs when the phone industry was being deregulated. In fact, in the early days of cable television, I had written and implemented tailor-made Action versus Reaction marketing plans for Cox Broadcasting, as they were acquiring cable TV franchises throughout the country. My reference list was starting to look pretty impressive, and that made it easier to get in the door.

As I got busier and busier, it became obvious that I was going to have to get a manager to take care of running my office while I was gone. I already had a secretary who was answering the phone and taking care of necessary paperwork, letters to dealers, reports, and so on, but it was time to expand.

# Chapter 7

## My Business Manager, Tom Wright—A Spiritual Man I Needed in My Life

One evening, as Dianne and I were attending my daughter Amy's college graduation party, Amy came up to me and said her roommate Sarah's dad, Tom, wanted to meet me. Tom Wright was one of the gentlest and mildest-mannered men I have ever met. He looked like a college professor and spoke like an English gentleman.

After the introduction, he said he heard I was a sales and management consultant and traveled the country doing motivational seminars. I explained it was a little more complicated than that, but he was close. He then said that Amy had mentioned I might be looking for a business manager. I responded that I was, and he asked if he could tell me a little about his background and perhaps be considered for the position.

Once he got the green light, he was on a roll. He started by telling me he went to New York City to study commercial art. He went on to explain he was young but married and needed income while going to school, so he took a job selling encyclopedias door-to-door. *Hmm,* I thought, *here is a guy with a healthy comfort zone.* I was impressed right away but asked how he ended up in Virginia Beach. The story really got interesting then. Tom was a very spiritual man and was being mentored by the assistant pastor at Dr. Norman Vincent Peale's church in New York City. I believe his ultimate goal was to become a minister. The pastor was friends with Pat Robertson, and Pat had asked if he knew anyone who would be qualified to be program director for the new Christian Broadcasting Network he was trying to build in Portsmouth, Virginia. Pat flew Tom there, and he was on a new mission. Commercial art was laid to rest.

The rest of the story seemed long but interesting, so I suggested he ride with me to Gatlinburg, Tennessee. I was the guest speaker for the National Speakers Association that year, and their headquarters were in Gatlinburg. I felt the ten-hour ride would let me know if Tom and I were compatible. Once we got in the car, Tom finished his story.

He had been offered a much higher paying position to help Jim and Tammy Bakker set up their new Charlotte-based Christian station and decided to move on. The rest was history. Jim Bakker started buffering himself from those he used to rely on for advice and soon was under investigation for criminal charges. Tom felt it best to distance himself and left. By the time he and I met, he had been selling home improvements and doing other meaningless jobs for a person of his experience.

It would have made most men very humbled, but when you're already a humble man of faith, you always know something is around the corner. There was.

I was impressed enough by his talents that I offered him the job. It was one of the best business decisions I ever made. With him running the office and making follow-up calls to clients, the company took on a whole new flow. I was free to improve on the programs I was teaching, and Tom made sure nothing was overlooked. I could see why Pat and Jim wanted him on their team.

Before long, I was on the road about twenty days a month and had frequent-flier miles with so many airlines that I was almost always able to fly first class. Fortunately, I was a nondrinker, so the free drinks weren't a big deal to me. Sometimes as they were passing out the booze, I would think, *Where were you folks when I needed you?* I know airline food gets a bad rap sometimes, but in first class, I always thought the meals were fine.

Any business traveler can tell horror stories about life on the road.

The divorce rate is very high for these nomadic and weary travelers. Many of those stories start off in dimly lit hotel cocktail lounges and end up in steamy hotel rooms where alcohol-fueled discussions of nagging husbands and wives become fodder for adulterous affairs. Fortunately for me, I was a nondrinker, so most of the stories I was able to avoid. Whenever I was in a town for two or more days, I made it a point to get in touch with Jack Horner for a chat and to be sure the allure of the road was kept at bay.

The most challenging thing for me was to keep from eating late-night room service meals followed by a huge dessert of the day, which always included ice cream and chocolate something or other. Of course, this meal plan always seemed to keep me awake half the night, and it was easy to gain weight. After learning the tricks of the road and gaining about ten pounds, I decided I better get back in some sort of shape. I once again started playing racquetball and tried to stay in reasonable physical condition. I would often seek out the nearest racquetball club in the town I was working in and could usually get a good workout.

# Chapter 8

## Challenges of Business Traveling and Family Life

As previously mentioned, I had met my wife, Dianne, in 1976, and by 1981, we had two sons of our own, Owen and Chad, to add to the previous family count. She had a daughter, Amy Marie, from a previous marriage, and I had a daughter and son, Amy Kathleen and Jason, from my previous marriage. Hmm, two Amys. What's the old saying? You can't make this stuff up. At any given moment, the joint was jumping.

In a committed relationship, it's easy to forget who goes through the most difficult part of the traveling experience. Business was excellent, and I was starting to make a good name for myself in the automobile industry. It seems with most things balance is required to keep successful. That was never one of my strong points.

Now that I was appearing before droves of "worshipers" of my wisdom and taking on celebrity status, I usually went to my room exhausted. After a hard day of motivational speaking and training salespeople from all over the country, I would immediately take a shower and then make my usual call home to check on Dianne and assure her that I loved and missed her terribly.

In the early traveling days, her response was, "Oh yes, and I miss you too." Then it became something like "Uh-huh, so when are you coming home?"

One of my favorite memories was a call I made from the Marriott in Phoenix. It went something like this.

"Hello, darlin'. How was your day?"

"Well, I just got home, and Amy Marie was here. She had got a call from your nine-year-old son, Chad, saying your eleven-year-old son, Owen, was trying to get in the house because your nine-year-old son, Chad, had locked him out. Chad said Owen was trying to kill him with the weed whacker and broke the door window because he wouldn't let him in."

"Hmmm," I grunted, and at that precise moment, room service knocked on the hotel door. "Hang on, honey. It's room service. Just put the steak over there please," I said. Not the right thing to say. I came back to a dial tone.

After my in-room dining, I called her back and found out they were fighting, as brothers do, and Owen was teasing and jerking Chad around. Nevertheless, with all this traveling I was doing, I needed to be more involved in all the boys' lives, including that of my oldest son, Jason, who lived with his mother and Amy Kathleen. It always bothered me that I never had a chance to be in his life on a day-to-day basis. I decided to make a few changes.

One of the decisions I made was to take temporary high-paying consulting positions with certain local dealers who knew my reputation, were anxious to have me come work with their sales team, and with whom I had done some action training in the past. Many of them were megadealers with more than one store, and they would often hire me to straighten out the neediest team. This would allow me to get off the road for a while and tend to being more of a parent. Dianne had paid her sole-parenting dues for a long time and liked the idea of me being close.

Working for someone else day in and day out was not my favorite thing to do. I liked the idea of working for myself. In addition, I enjoyed the traveling, teaching, and motivating, but the present times seemed to call for it.

# Chapter 9

## Florida Client Is Calling—"Make Me an Offer I Can't Refuse"

One of my largest clients was in a small southwestern Florida town called Punta Gorda. It is part of Charlotte County, Florida. Punta Gorda is Spanish for "Fat Point." History tells us it was visited by Ponce de León, and there is a statue erected at one of the coastal parks. All I knew was that it was one of the most beautiful places in the world, and for about seven months out of the year, it was heaven. The other five months you just sort of hung on through the heat and possible hurricanes or went north as so many did. They were referred to as snowbirds. They usually started flocking in around late October and flying back north in late April or May.

Most of the local economy was directly affected by the season change. Sunshine Automotive was the largest car dealer in the county and perhaps in the entire southwestern part of Florida. They were what is commonly referred to as a localized "megadealer," in other words, they had multiple new-car franchises at one location. They had been on the Action versus Reaction and Winning Edge programs for over a year, and we had increased their production and profit by about 30 percent. This would translate into millions of dollars, and understandably they were one of my biggest fans.

Around March of 1994, Sunshine was looking for ways to expand their dealerships. The idea was to create a mall concept that would take up two full blocks on the main street in the heart of Punta Gorda.

They had looked within the organization for someone to be the general sales manager (GSM) but felt it would be best to go outside the organization and try to entice me to take the position. The present GSM was a good guy, but I assumed he was being eased out of the position because they felt he might not be the guy for the future. This would not be a consulting contract; it would be a job, albeit potentially a very well-paying job. I thought to myself, *Hmmm, with the strides they've already made using our system, if I was there every day, we could really light it up.*

In spite of the income potential and beautiful surroundings, when I got the offer, my first reaction was negative. I had apprehension about giving up my business and going back to work for someone else. I started weighing the pros and cons and used the formula given to me by Jack Horner regarding major decisions. He suggested removing fear and guilt from all decisions and just listing the real pluses and minuses.

I considered Dianne's words of years before: "If I ever moved anywhere from Virginia Beach, it would only be to Florida." I considered the uprooting of the boys in their young teenage years and how it might affect them. I considered giving up my freedom and how much that meant to me. Then Dianne and I talked.

She was apprehensive about the change. We had gotten to a point where we were both relatively stable and Owen and Chad were doing well in school and their respective sports, Owen's BMX and surfing and Chad's soccer and wrestling. As I mentioned, life was good. But I was still traveling more than either of us wanted, and this seemed like an ideal opportunity. It was also in beautiful South Florida. I told Mickey the CEO and part owner I would let him know. He then called me back and said, "The majority owners who founded the company would like to invite you and Dianne to spend a week at their condo on Boca Grande Island. It will be a good place for you to think about it."

It isn't an exaggeration to proclaim Boca Grande as one of the most beautiful places in the world. The beaches are pristine white and soft as talcum powder, a perfect place to think about something. It's also famous for its tarpon fishing and both President Bushes came each year to fish and enjoy the relaxing atmosphere. We figured, what the heck? Let's at least take a vacation if nothing else, and then we can look around the community and see what we think.

By this time, Dianne and I were both golfers, and after playing at a few fancy South Florida courses and loving the beach, we had made our decision. It was time to talk money and then tell the kids.

Mickey, the CEO, was good with expenses but didn't seem to have very good people skills, and I got the feeling he didn't really care. He would be the first to tell you, "That's why I've got you." I knew this going into the negotiations and tried to prepare myself. The first thing I thought of was, *In order for me to make this commitment to sell my consulting business, I will need some sort of contract with Sunshine.* By this time, I had my entire training program on video and sold the videos across the country so they were a major source of income for me. I had also hired a couple of fellows from different parts of the country to work with me. I called them my associates. In fact, the legal name of my corporation was and still is Gene Gorman and Associates Inc. One of those associates, Paul Nalle, was eager to buy the rights to my videos and client list if I ever decided to sell.

Contracts with employees were not very common in the car business in those days, and I knew this. In fact, with all of my Winning Edge clients, I never signed anything more than a one-visit contract, payable after the workshop was done. I used to tell dealers, "If what I'm teaching your sales team isn't making you more money instantly, you shouldn't have me back." They really liked that idea, and I did too. Mickey knew this from our past experience, and I assumed he would become defensive if I mentioned a contract, but this was a little different. I told Mickey that we had decided to accept the offer from Sunshine as long as they would move us and take care of any and all expenses to get us to Florida. He agreed.

My confidence was at an all-time high, so in addition, I asked that he show me the old general sales manager's (GSM) pay plan and that he draw me up a pay plan exactly like that of the guy I was replacing. If I did a better job, I'd make more money than he did, and if I did a worse job, he could fire me. He chuckled but liked that idea and agreed to it immediately. He broke out the present GSM's pay plan, and the only concern I had and I felt the need to ask the question was, "Are you sure you want to pay me on gross profit and not net?"

He was quick to respond, "You make the gross, Gorman, and I'll take care of the expenses."

*Hmmm, a little unusual,* I thought, *but that sounds good to me.*

The moving vans arrived right after the kids got out of school in mid-June 1994. I had negotiated with Paul to buy my business, but just in case things didn't work out financially as quickly as I anticipated, I held mutual rights to the sale of video and audio tapes. Dianne sold or gave away most of our beautiful Queen Anne furniture and anxiously awaited the tropical-theme shopping sprees for our new house once we arrived in Punta Gorda. But there was one more thing I had to do before leaving for Florida.

The combat experience and hospitalization from injuries incurred while in Vietnam seemed to always hover in my mind. Regardless of the success I was enjoying, I seemed to have this underlying sense of survivor's guilt that wouldn't go away. As previously mentioned, I had tried to drown the memories with booze, all to no avail. In 1994, Lawrence Maddry, a journalist with the local *Virginian Pilot* news-paper did a story on Frank Hardy, a marine who died saving my life during a combat operation in Vietnam. The details are spelled out in the article I've included as an insert in this book.

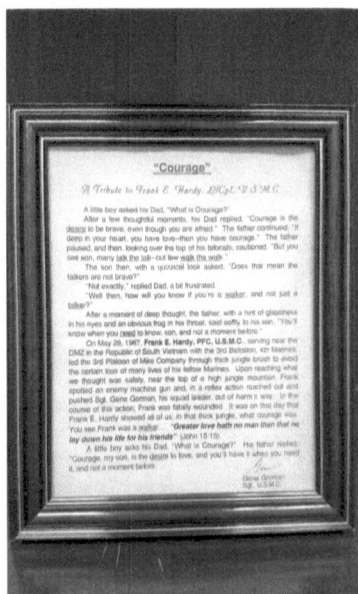

Frank's newspaper article

As you will see, the experience spelled out in this article gave me a sense of closure, and I was finally able to move on.

Our great Florida adventure could now begin.

Our home was a modest yet comfortable house situated on a large canal that led to the Peace River, which would quickly take you to the Gulf of Mexico. All of our neighbors had huge boats that could easily motor or sail to anywhere in the world, and some of them did during the summer months. *Forbes* magazine rated it the best small town in America that year, and it would be hard to find a better place to live than Punta Gorda. The climate was ideal for seven months out of the year, and the entire town was surrounded by water and golf courses, perfect for retired folks but not so interesting for teenage boys. It would be important to get Owen and Chad involved in something as soon as possible. Idle minds are not ideal for young people, and it would be late August before school started.

My new position wouldn't start until July 1, so I had a couple of weeks to honor my commitment to the boys to get a boat. Since none of us had any boating experience, I made a deal with Owen. If he and his mom would take a local Coast Guard Auxiliary course and complete it, I would buy a boat. Chad was too young to take the course, and Dianne was not really interested in learning how to run a boat, but she agreed. Three weeks later, after their successful graduation from the course on how to navigate a boat, we bought a little eighteen-foot motorboat, and you would have thought we had purchased the *Titanic*.

We proudly sailed the harbor that first day and promptly ran aground about three times until we figured out how to avoid some of the very shallow waters of the Peace River. As we sat idle, we were dwarfed by the neighbor's monster boats passing by. They raised their eyebrows with a sad look of pity on us poor beginners. We looked like the aquatic version of the Beverly hillbillies.

# Chapter 10

## Megadealer—Sunshine Automotive: Turning the Deal Around

One of the first things I had to do at Sunshine Automotive was create an atmosphere of harmony, when three of the managers on my staff felt like they should have been the ones who got my new job. Their attitude, as well as the eye-rolling camaraderie with their sales staffs when in my presence, made it apparent I was going to have to start with a firm line of who was in charge, without sabotaging their effectiveness.

I had learned that it is more important people know where you stand than like where you stand. I decided to do a one-on-one meeting with each of them.

I offered a bit of compassion for all of the change taking place, followed by assurance that negativity would not be tolerated, and said if any of them felt like they couldn't abide by these guidelines, I understood and would understand them leaving. But if they choose to stay, it would have to be on my terms and to achieve our goals, it must be done with leaders who were positive and enthusiastic. I gave them all forty-eight hours to think about it. They all chose to stay. Now my job was to earn their respect.

Our sales team was made up of twenty-five to thirty salespeople, and they were averaging about 280 cars per month. My personal goal was to take the organization to 500 sales per month and increase the per-sale profit. My research had shown we were losing a great deal of business to the other same-name-brand franchise dealers in Ft. Myers and Venice, twenty-two miles away in each direction, although our county was one of the fastest growing in the country and was the fastest-growing retirement county in the United States.

My experience had shown me that in order to reach 500 sales per month, we were going to need fifty salespeople on staff and five constantly in training. Not an easy task in little old Punta Gorda. At our first sales meeting, I announced to the entire organization my plans to double the sales staff and the grumbling was unanimous. I noticed some of the sales managers looking around the room and grinning with what seemed like a "How do you like Ol' Clean Gene now" look. During my training with them in the past, they all heard the story of the old used-car boys and my nickname of "Clean Gene." It was now time to do a one-on-one meeting with the salespeople.

I explained to each one of them what was going to be required daily, weekly, and monthly. Furthermore, I told them I understood if they couldn't go along with it, but if they choose to stay and work harder, they would all make more money. I also gave them all two weeks to think about it, unless their attitude became negative, and then I would make the decision for them. Since I had been working with Sunshine as a consultant for some time, they knew the basics of the program. They just didn't realize the accountability that was going to be demanded of them with me on location every day. I knew that was going to make some of them nervous. It also made me a bit nervous. After two weeks, they all stayed. Hallelujah!

Mickey pretty much let me do my thing with the sales team, and that was a good thing. Once a week, we would have a meeting with the comptroller and general service manager to review inventory and talk about certain decisions that needed to be made as a management team, but sales and finance was my baby. Within three months, we were on target to reach our goal. I had to change the finance manager's bonus plan a bit because they were being paid bonuses based on a very average job. All I did was research the average success numbers from all of the dealers in Florida and required our finance managers to be in the top 10 percent to receive any bonuses. They never missed their bonus, made more money, and took greater pride in a job well done. Amazing, all we had to do was raise the bar, and they reached it. Long before, I had learned mediocrity can become the norm if you let it. The comfort zone was alive and well.

As part of my daily routine, I made it a point to walk the entire two blocks twice a day, physically shaking hands or patting everyone on the back. This would take about an hour and a half each trip, but with fifteen different franchises, it was the most important thing I could do. I surmised that my most important role was to keep a positive attitude circulating throughout the entire organization. The system was in place, and my daily and weekly reports would constantly tell me what was working and what needed attention. Any reprimanding was to be done in private. I knew I could only expect what I inspected so everyone knew at any moment the boss might be walking in the door. It was working and working very well.

By month 4, we were starting to roll. We had our annual car show in the fall, and with the early return of some of the snowbirds, I felt like this could be our five hundred month. The tension rose as we moved closer and closer, and the vibes in the whole organization were rising. Five hundred cars in little Punta Gorda would mean we finally started getting back the business we had been losing to the surrounding markets and making a statement as to the new big dog in southwest Florida. In the car business, there is an old saying that the best time to sell a car is right after you sold one. You're pumped up and feel invincible, and confidence is oozing out of every pore in your body. Multiply that times forty-five to fifty salespeople, and you can imagine the energy. I guess it's like the physics law that a body in motion tends to stay in motion and a body at rest tends to stay at rest. Well, we had a bunch of bodies in motion.

I think the final tally was over 550. Every one of my managers congratulated me as I did them, and the salespeople were now unanimous in believing we were the best and they really could do more than they ever believed they could. That was where my joy came. Damn, I felt good.

Mickey didn't seem to share the same enthusiasm as everyone

else in the company about our record-breaking numbers. I wasn't sure why but had my suspicions. I was to find out at the next management meeting. It seemed that all of the managers had hit all of the bonuses available to them and were on track to do it again now that they knew they could do it and the Winning Edge was in full bloom. This meant that the company made more gross profit than they ever had made, but the percent of profit to sales could be lower than the industry standard even though we still made more net profit. Of course, that might mean when Mickey went to the next dealer Twenty Group meeting, he would have to explain why his management and sales commission percentages were so high. Mickey was used to being the expense-controlling king, and now he might have to explain to his peers how it got out of control. There's that damn ego again.

It seemed Mickey's solution was going to be simple, put a 10 percent surcharge on each manager's gross profit, which would greatly affect their pay. When he mentioned this to me, I was a bit taken aback. "How am I going to go to the managers who have done the best job ever and congratulate them with, 'You've done a great job, and for your reward, we're going to cut your pay?'"

The other two managers in the meeting offered no help. Hell, all of my sales managers were making more money than they were. Mickey's response was "Don't worry, Gorman; I'm not surcharging your pay."

I said, "If you surcharge theirs, you've got to surcharge mine." I walked out of the office, shaking my head and went to break the news to my managers. I thought about Mickey's original decision to pay everyone on gross instead of net and how important it is to structure pay plans properly up front, so good jobs are rewarded in a balanced yet positive way, a necessity to maintaining momentum in a sales operation.

I was so angry at the changing of the deal that I almost quit. I had seen dealers go down similar roads before, and it always came back to bite them. For some reason, the power of good systems and leadership is easily underestimated.

When I broke the news to the guys, they shrugged and said,

"That's typical." They knew Mickey. I assured them we all were going to be sharing in the surcharge. I did my best to keep them pumped up and full steam ahead but knew it would take a while for them to recover. When I got home, I shared the news with Dianne, and she encouraged me to shake it off and not do anything impulsively. It went something like this.

"We can't let this disrupt our home. My God, you're still making more money than you've ever made in your life."

My response was "Yeah, but I can't trust that guy, and I don't know if I can work for someone I can't trust."

Her logical thinking of course was "Here we are living in Florida, boys are doing great in school, and you are going to quit your job and go back on the road."

I saw the fear in her eyes and assured her I would stay put and see how things looked in ninety days.

Thank God Harold, one of my spiritual mentors, was only a phone call away. I could always bounce these types of situations off of him, and he would always go back to the simple philosophy of "Show up and trust God. He'll show you what to do at just the right time."

The next day, I went back to work with new resolve, committed to controlling what I could control and not worrying about things I couldn't. That was the message I presented to my managers, and they seemed to agree. "Let's take the surcharge, accept it, and blow the lid off the goals," regardless of the new surcharge. They regained their enthusiasm, and before long, we were back to clicking along in record fashion.

# Chapter 11

## Breeding the Next Generation— Kids in Business, Does It Work?

B y this time, my son Owen was fifteen, doing well in school, and starting to show signs of a little business acumen. One day, while visiting me at work, he ran into the guy who did the pin-striping on our cars as well as door-edge guards and little detailing jobs around the dealership. The next thing I knew, he had been hired by that guy and was asking me if it would be okay for him to start working after school to make himself some extra cash. I smiled and started beaming a bit with dad pride. "Of course," I answered, and that was that. The next thing I knew, he had written out a small business plan and was now an entrepreneur. I thought, *Hmmm, I guess my early intuition about him was right.* I always felt like he had that intensity the leaders have. The following year, he was getting out of school early on some learn and work program, and his teachers, I learned later, were amazed at his work ethic. Little did I know, someday he would be running our entire organization.

Chad had just started middle school and as usual was making all A's and everybody loved him. Sadly soccer and wrestling were not offered in the middle schools. Once the high school wrestling coaches found out about his scholastic wrestling prowess in Virginia Beach, they talked him and a few of the other middle school kids into coming over to the high school to work out with the team. Eventually, he would go on to become a high school all American.

By then, the entire sales team had accepted the new terms and we had continued to grow and grow as a company. Over the next six months, volume and profit had continued to increase. In fact, my annual personal income had gotten very substantial. It was true that we were all working our fannies off, but we were all making a lot of money for sleepy Ol' Punta Gorda, Florida. Even I was amazed at how well the program was working. I guess Harold was right.

It was August 1995 when Mickey called me privately into his office and informed me he was going to have to adjust everyone's pay again. When I reminded him that everybody's earnings were based on their pay plan and my earnings were based on the original deal we made a year before, his comment was "Jesus Christ, Gorman, you're making more money than me."

Ah, so that was the real issue. I told him that I didn't have a problem with that. Using the Dallas Cowboys football team as an example, I replied, "Emmett Smith makes more money than Coach Jimmie Johnson." I also pointed out the company was more profitable than it had ever been. He wasn't impressed and told me that he was going to have to take my company car away from me and make me pay my own insurance. I was totally blown away.

Almost every car dealer in the industry provided a demo for their general sales manager, and many with organizations as large as ours provided one for their spouses as well. In addition, it would be a bit embarrassing. All of the other salespeople and managers knew a car was automatic for any GSM. It felt like a slap in the face, and I just didn't understand the business logic. I was disappointed, shook my head, and walked out the door. Then I got angry. "God damn ego-maniac," I whispered to myself.

# Chapter 12

## The Ninety-Day Wait—Magical Solution for Relationships

Early on in our marriage and after a few futile shouting matches, Dianne and I made a commitment regarding disagreements. Whenever we were at odds with each other about something, we would each take a separate car, meet at a quiet public restaurant with a list of the things that bothered us about the other person, and let the other person know. We wouldn't debate who was wrong; we would just share what was bothering us about the other person. Some of the issues seemed big at the time and rather than just breaking up, we agreed to put the list aside for ninety days and meet again to see if the issues had been resolved. The other person could change, call it a deal breaker, and make a decision or accept what was on the list and vice versa.

Over thirty-eight years of marriage, we've probably had five of these sit-downs. We never had to go back and rehash the previous issues, and most of the time, we had either changed or forgotten what was on the list. The next six months were going to present the relationship with our biggest challenge yet.

After leaving Mickey's office, I wandered around in a state of shock. I just didn't understand why this guy would jeopardize the company's success by this type of action. I called Harold. He suggested that maybe because of ego he was trying to ease me out or maybe he had miscalculated how successful I could make the company and couldn't handle me being the fair-haired boy. Either way, I was going to have to make a decision. He then reassured me that God was going to take care of me no matter which way I decided to go. Harold was easy. Next, I had to tell Dianne what I was thinking.

When I got home that night, Dianne could see by my face I was troubled. Finally, I told her what went on that day. As usual, she looked for the pony in this pile of horse manure and said, "Aren't we lucky we have the money to buy a car?" She saw the dollar and commonsense logic of it all, but deep in her heart, she knew this was a potential deal breaker. I told her I just didn't know if I could work for this guy. She cried, and I held her and said not to worry. Whatever I did, we'd be okay. It was obvious the situation was scaring the hell out of her; she got a bit feisty and said, "We are not moving back to Virginia." I tried to reassure her and told her I hadn't decided what I was going to do yet. Understandably she was concerned about uprooting the boys and losing our lifestyle and all the other good stuff that can come with making big bucks.

Things were testy around our house, and it was obvious Dianne was settling into a depression. She was filled with that feeling of impending doom, and I was concerned about her. In the final analysis, I agreed to buy a car and try to hang on for ninety more days and see how I felt, but deep down, I knew I was going to have a hard time staying and working with Mickey. I thought of the many clients I had consulted over the years who had made similar decisions that almost destroyed their companies and never could quite understand it.

With the help of Harold's spiritual perspective on things, I was able to keep my attitude upbeat, and business was rolling along at record levels. Almost every day since I first met Jack Horner, I've started my day with a prayer and going into my trance, asking to be moved to do what God's will was for me. With my continued day-to-day interaction with Mickey, it became more and more difficult to go to work and look him in the eye. By November of 1995, I had decided I was going to resign and go back on the road.

I didn't tell Dianne right away. I figured I would wait until the time was upon us. This would be very difficult for our family, but after a lot of prayer and trances, I felt like I was being drawn to take some sort of action.

It was pretty standard for the managers to get a substantial bonus on December 15. My year-end bonus was expected to be huge. In spite of the fact it had been about four months since the last pay plan adjustment and company car loss, I felt December 1 would be a good time to resign. I was still very angry and wanted Mickey to know that I was not going to be held hostage by a Christmas bonus and this was really about the trust in him I had lost. My timing and words were such that everyone was caught by surprise. After all, things were good, and you would think the blow to my ego would have long been forgotten, but it hadn't.

I walked into Mickey's office when he was alone and was greeted by the standard, "Hello, Gene O."

I sat down and without any hesitation said, "I've decided to resign and thought I would tell you before bonus time so you can give me or not give me whatever you feel is fair for the job I've done."

The shock on his face was obvious, and his next words were "Have you talked this over with Dianne?"

I assured him we had discussed this at great length, but this was my decision and no one else's. I then let him know that no one else knew and I would keep this quiet until he wanted to announce it. He asked if I had given this a lot of thought, and I said, "I've been thinking about this for quite some time." I stood up and told him I would go on with business as usual until he decided how he wanted to handle the announcement. I walked out the door. When I turned the corner, I was overwhelmed with gratitude and a resounding sense of self-esteem. I think I was even smiling. Perhaps I was delusional, but God, I felt free.

A couple of days later, Mickey called me into his office and said the announcement would take place at the sales meeting on December 15. I mentioned it to no one until that morning. After the meeting, no explanation was necessary from me and no one asked. They all knew and most of them were probably amazed I stayed on as long as I did. In fairness, Mickey did give me a prorated bonus, perhaps trying to get me to reconsider. I could tell he had some concerns about the future by the look in his eyes, but I was done and there would be no going back.

My last order of business and one of my most gratifying meetings with Mickey was recommending my replacement. Mickey called me into his office, where we were joined by the comptroller and the general service manager.

I sat down, and they asked me if I thought anyone who was presently with the company would be able to do my job. Most of the guys who had wanted my job previously were being considered, but I suggested Tonya Blair, the female used-car manager, who wasn't even on their list. They rolled their eyes a bit and were a little taken aback. They discussed the fact she was extremely heavy and didn't have the image they were looking for. I assured them that heavy or not, she was still very neat, extremely organized, and the most loyal and knowledgeable person they had. They fought me on this image thing for some time but finally relented, and Tonya is still the general sales manager at this writing, some twenty years later. By December 25, 1995, I was gone.

It was no surprise to me that Mickey was gone shortly after I left, and the company went back to doing things the way they were doing them before my arrival. Interestingly enough, the comptroller and general service manager were gone shortly thereafter as well.

Now what was I going to do?

When I got home that night, Dianne was barely speaking to me. I had told her the previous day what my plan was, and even though she didn't agree with me, I felt I needed to let her know before anyone else. I assured her that something good was going to come up, and worst-case scenario, I was going to have to go back on the road and teach my beloved Action versus Reaction and Winning Edge programs. For some reason, my faith was strong.

I never doubted my success capabilities. My faith in God was strong, and even though I might be gone three or four nights a week, I felt we would be able to maintain our present lifestyle. I vowed I would never put myself into a position where someone else could decide my fate again. Her biggest concern was my sharing in the raising of two teenage boys, an understandable concern.

# Chapter 13

## Gene Gorman Auto Sales—
## Time to Become a Dealer

As I was driving home the day of my resignation, heading toward Fort Myers to try to book some local dealers for workshops, I noticed a guy putting up a "For Sale or Lease" sign on a deserted lot about a half mile south of Sunshine Automotive. Just the day before, it had been a recreational vehicle sales and service business. I turned in sharply, introduced myself to a guy named John, and asked him how much he was asking for the place. He told me he worked for the owner but was charged with getting it ready for sale. The buy figure seemed reasonable, but I couldn't commit to buying because I didn't have a job, so I said, "Do you think he would lease it with a first right of refusal to buy in a year?" He said the owner lived in Naples, about forty miles south, and preferred to sell it but would lease it for the right price.

After he told me the monthly lease price, I suggested it was a bit high, but I was willing to take a look at it. Like most career car salespeople, off and on in my automotive career, I had dreamed of owning my own little dealership and had even drawn up a business plan a couple of years earlier. Now timing was even more of an issue.

There were two buildings and a tall garage on the lot. One building was a sales office and the other was a parts department. Surprisingly, all of the equipment, furniture, phones, fax machines, and computers were still exactly where the previous tenant had left them. In fact, all of the used parts, refrigerators, and toilets were still on site. By law, any of those items had to go to a dump and you would have to pay extra to dump the items that used chemicals as part of their operation. Damn, I never knew toilets broke down so much in RVs. There must have been thirty to forty of them on site. The previous tenant had gone broke, left everything, and headed out of town.

My mind and my adrenaline started racing. The rent fit my business plan formula, and the location was perfect. It was only two miles from my house and near the kids' schools. I thought, *Hmm, this place is ready to do business right now. All I need to do is clean it up, get a license, buy some cars, and get rocking.* Realizing John was probably anxious to get the deal done quickly so he wouldn't have to unload this mess that had been left, I blurted, "I'll tell you what I'll do. If your owner will let me have the place just as it is right now, equipment and everything, and give me first right of refusal to buy within a year, I'll give you one month's rent and an equal security deposit right now, and you won't have to worry about anything."

His eyes got big, and he said he would get back to me in a couple of hours. That was how long it took to get to Naples and talk to the owner.

I didn't dare call Dianne yet but immediately headed out to look at what kind of cars the other used-car dealers were carrying and started making notes. I already had my plan; now all I had to do was my research and market analysis and then get the ball rolling. I waited impatiently for the call. As promised, John called me and excitedly said the owner would do the deal and would be glad to sell me all the furnishings and equipment with a separate contract at a very reasonable price. I cautiously informed him that if that was the case, I would just get my own equipment and furniture and if we could adjust the lease price down a bit, we had a deal. I reminded him he was going to have to unload all this equipment and then clean the place up and get rid of the chemical item expense. He said, "Let me work on him a bit."

Within another hour, he said he was on his way with a lease and to pick up the rent and deposit. Wow, I was almost a car dealer. Now to tell Dianne.

The approach I used with Dianne was to try to get her as excited as I was about this newest adventure. She did her best to be positive but was still smarting from the resignation and financial fear. I told her that once I got my license, I would be able to stay home and wouldn't have to travel. Until then, I would have to go back on the road doing workshops, but it would be temporary. She tried to believe me but knew how much I loved to train and motivate, and I would have to prove to her I was sincere. I understood that.

Over the course of the next few weeks, I was busy going to dealer school and submitting applications for all of the various licenses, zoning permits, bonds, and so on to be a car dealer. An exhausting time period was to follow, and it took about three months before I was able to start selling cars. Dianne became very supportive in that time frame, and I explained to her that I needed her levelheadedness to do my marketing research. Armed with the fact I had already signed the lease, she joined me on trips to visit other dealers outside of our market area to find out some of the tips on how to be successful. I had talked to some of my Sunshine suppliers, who were glad to have me as a new client, and they referred me to certain successful dealers around the state I could learn from. I discovered all you have to do is reassure them you're going to be opening out of their market and tell them that so-and-so said they were an excellent dealer and maybe they would be good people to learn from. Once flattered, they usually tell you everything. Successful people are never afraid to share ideas because they know most people aren't willing to do what it takes to be successful. We both learned a lot on these trips.

Now, all I needed was to get some money to buy some cars. I had excellent credit by this time and felt sure with the great business plan I had drawn up, any bank would love to get me as a client. I even drew up an investor letter to make sure they would be confident I knew what I was doing. Furthermore, this was a unique opportunity for them to get in on the ground floor of this new enterprise. It may have been the finest proposal I have ever done.

It included my high-powered résumé and a complete marketing plan. As usual, my enthusiasm far exceeded reality. I was turned down by everybody. All of the banks flattered me on my business plan, and many said they had never seen one quite as well done, followed by "We only finance new-car dealers, but we wish you well on your new enterprise." It was a familiar story, I concluded. The banks would only lend money to the people who didn't need the money.

I was taken aback a bit but recharged by the rejection. Hell, I'd been down more difficult roads than this. Besides, I had great credit and credit card companies loved me. Within a month, I had enough credit lines to buy as many cars as I needed; now all I had to do was sell the cars and pay them off quickly. This really got Dianne's anxiety level rising, but her faith never wavered. We were car dealers.

Even though it took until April to start selling cars, in January of 1996, we were licensed as Gene Gorman and Associates Inc., doing business as Gene Gorman Auto Sales.

# Chapter 14

## Into Action—The Ol' Competitive Spirit Never Dies

Tom Wright, my former agent and business manager, and I had stayed close over the past year and a half. Once I got licensed, he asked if there was anything he could do in Florida to help me get set up. I told him I would need a lot of help setting things up the way I liked them and because he was familiar with my style of business, he could come down from Virginia and join me. I assured him I could pay him well, but he would have to get his own place to live. He decided to make a trip down and evaluate the possibilities. Within a week, he was on the scene.

The former parts building used to have an apartment in the back room. It was now used for storage but had a kitchen and bathroom as well as a living area and small bedroom. It was ideal for anyone who wanted to take the time to do a bit of decorating. Tom was a wizard at that, and within a week, he had himself quite a neat little apartment. Now, how about getting rid of all those toilets and refrigerators?

Now that I had everything in place and Tom had himself a comfortable lifestyle, it was time to go buy some cars. In my analysis, I noticed that no one in my market had any imports. I reasoned that with my background in selling imports, this might be a niche I could capture while my competitors were sleeping. Gene Gorman Auto Sales could stock about thirty cars comfortably, so I went to the nearest auction and stocked up on Toyotas, Hondas, and Nissans, with a few domestic cars just to fill up the vacant spaces on the lot. I was amazed at how many were available. Yep, I was going to be the new import king. With my expertise and Tom's loyalty, we should hit the ground running. After sixty days, we still had all of those imports and the only cars we were selling in little old Punta Gorda were the domestic cars. I had foolishly supposed I could make a market where none existed—one of the lessons I learned in the first year. There would be many more.

The problem was most of our market was made up of retirees, and in 1996, they were still very anti-import. The younger markets, like Virginia Beach, didn't have the Pearl Harbor resentment these old folks had. Now I knew why our competitors didn't carry any imports. Before long, I was taking the imports back to the auction to be bought by dealers from the younger markets of Florida, like Orlando, Tampa, Miami, and Jacksonville. I then stocked up on Chrysler Fifth Avenues, Ford Crown Victorias, and all of the Mercury Grand Marquis I could find. Once filled with the right inventory, business took off. My old competitive spirit came back. Now to find out what the top guys' numbers were. I guess the old competitive drive never leaves you.

I will be forever grateful for Tom Wright's help in getting set up. He has one of those demeanors that makes everyone he is around feel more at peace and no matter what's going on, everything's going to be all right. He was a man of tremendous faith and a stabilizing force for my sometimes high-energy personality. Unfortunately, he couldn't stay with me after those first few months because of family needs back in Virginia, and I had to say farewell to him. I hired a few other guys to fill in when I went to the auctions to buy more cars, but no one could take the place of my dear old friend. To this day, we stay in touch. He is retired at this writing and doing well.

In order not to make the same mistake I made in the beginning, I decided I would invest in a monthly report that showed exactly what every dealer, new and used, was selling within twenty-five miles of my market and carry the hottest-selling products. We then expanded the information request to include all of southwest Florida. It became an invaluable report, and Owen and I review it monthly to this day. It tells us what is selling—i.e., year, make, model, and mileage—what banks are financing, and the sex and age of all of the customers. This allows us to target our advertising and carry the right inventory. By the end of the first year, we were the number-one volume independent dealer in our county and sold more used cars than almost all of the new-car franchises. At this writing, we have grown to be the number-one volume independent used-car dealer in all of southwest Florida and have been for over twenty years. Interestingly enough, the banks started seeking my business and making me proposals. This has held true for the past fifteen years but not without some interesting challenges along the way.

# Chapter 15

## Dianne Becomes My Partner—"I'd Give 'Em Away, but My Wife Won't Let Me"

After considerable begging from me, Dianne had become our comptroller, and I decided to use the slogan "I'd give 'em away, but my wife won't let me."

Slogan

I picked the slogan up in my travels from a guy in California named "Mad Man" Earl Muntz. He was a wild and crazy character and often flew a small plane with a banner trailing behind it using that same slogan. I didn't have a plane, but it seemed apropos for our structure and was a huge hit in our marketplace. I also decided I would put my picture on all of our signs so people would know there was a real, live human being they could talk to if they had a problem. I felt that would be a plus when people were buying a used car. In addition, I believe it created a relationship with everyone in the community who drove by our dealership. In the first few years, while our kids were very active in school sports and clubs, their friends used to always comment, "Oh your mom is the one that won't let your dad give 'em away," and customers invariably would say to me, "Let me talk to your wife." The slogan was and is a big part of our local identity.

Just a side note, after my son Owen graduated from high school, he went on to Edison College and Florida Gulf Coast University to study psychology. He had been a large part of our company in the last couple of years of high school, handling all of the inventory and detailing needs but wanted to go on to college. I encouraged him to follow his dreams, and if he wanted to become part of the business, it would be here for him.

After completing his education, Owen came to me and said he finally realized he loved the car business and told me he wanted to learn everything he could about the money-making end of it. I was elated and could use his help full-time.

He caught on quick to buying and appraising cars, and before long, I felt it was time to send him to the highly acclaimed Jim Moran Finance and Insurance School. They were one of the top-rated automotive finance, warranty, and insurance companies in the nation. I had maintained my relations with them after leaving Sunshine, and I believe Owen was the only used-car dealer representative in the school.

It was a demanding school but necessary for anyone who planned on moving up in the car business. He was by far the youngest guy in the class and had no experience in automotive finance, but his gift was always numbers. Furthermore, he grew up in the car business so he knew more about the overall business than most of the people in the class, in spite of his youth. He became one of the class stars. I was super proud of him. He immediately went to work, buying most of our cars. Within a couple more years, he had bought some property and a nice home and had a beautiful redheaded wife named—believe it or not—Aimee. That made three Amys in our family. It could sometimes get confusing.

As a proud father and also as the CEO of our corporation, I am happy to say, in 2010, Owen was promoted to vice president and general manager of our entire operation. Understandably, he is paid on gross profit minus expenses he has control over. Any pay cuts he experiences will be brought on by him. He buys all of the cars and does all of the hiring and firing for the entire operation. In addition, he ensures the Action versus Reaction Management, Action versus Reaction Selling, Ten Steps to Success, and Winning Edge programs are in place in each operation.

# Chapter 16

## Hurricane Charley Destroys Almost Everything but … No Victims Allowed

By 2004, we were well on our way to having our best year ever. We had been the number-one independent dealer in our county every month for eight straight years, selling more used vehicles than almost all of the new-car franchises and had repeatedly maintained a net profit of over 20 percent net to gross each year, a very high margin considering the benchmarks in our industry.

I guess you could say we were clicking along pretty well. One of our newest ventures was adding a new location about a hundred yards down from our original one. We called it Gorman Family Motors. After a short while, we formed our own finance company, Gene Gorman Financial Inc., and started financing some of our own cars rather than putting the contracts with a bank or a small loan company. In many places, this is referred to as buy here, pay here, or BHPH. As in most communities, a certain segment of the people were in need of a reliable car at a fair price but were burdened by bad credit in their past and no banks would touch them.

The small loan companies would charge ridiculous interest rates, and that never sat well with me. I had been in these customers' position in the past during my drunken crazy days and thought I could do better for them and at the same time make a fair profit.

We use a scoring sheet when we decide who can qualify for how much car or truck, and I'm pleased to say that often our interest rates are 10 percent less than they could get anywhere else and that makes me feel good. Since most of these folks are families, I thought the name Gene Gorman Family Motors might make them feel more comfortable. It seemed to work because it caught on instantly. The vehicles we sell these customers are not typical BHPH cars. Most of them have a warranty and have been checked out extensively to ensure they will keep running. People with bad credit will pay if the car keeps running. Most people with bad credit are good people who have fallen on hard times or made some bad decisions in their past and are now trying to get back on their feet. I guess you could say we were trying to help people yet still make some money. In fact, because of our unique scoring sheet, our delinquency rate is generally lower than any of the lenders we do business with. Business was good at both of our locations, and we were optimistic about the future.

On Friday, August 13, 2004, a category-4 hurricane ripped through our community and literally destroyed the town. Hurricane Charley was supposed to go north toward Tampa, but because of a sudden shift in the wind current, it took a hard right turn and tore through Punta Gorda before heading inland and going north. The eye of the storm passed directly over our neighborhood and business community with winds in excess of 170 miles per hour. Both of our car lots were destroyed, and the inventories at both locations were devastated by wind and debris.

Most of our cars were totaled, and the remainder suffered massive damage. In addition, every home in the town was terribly damaged with roofs torn off as well as windows and frames completely warped and twisted. Some homes were leveled. My son Jason, who was visiting at the time, was home with me, and we watched as our roof disappeared, our windows and doors were bent and twisted by the pressure, and our lanai was torn out to be carried away to someplace still unknown. Owen was at his home with Aimee, and they suffered the same consequences. Power lines were down everywhere, and we would be without power for about ten days. Fortunately Dianne was in Virginia when the storm hit and Chad was at the University of Florida in Gainesville.

When the storm finally passed, Jason and I got into a four-wheel-drive truck I had taken home and started working our way toward the dealerships to survey the damage. We figured we would check a few of the surrounding retirement neighborhoods to see if anyone needed any emergency help before we headed to the car lots. Some of the seniors were walking around in shock, but no one needed our help.

When we got to the dealerships, it seemed obvious we were going to be out of business for a long time. As we walked around behind the sales office, a tender moment occurred. It suddenly hit me that all this work we had done for so many years was gone in a flash. I stood there, surveying the damage, and became overwhelmed with sadness at the lost homes of my employees as well as the hard work that seemed to be all for naught.

I couldn't help myself and started sobbing. Jason came to my side and put his arm around my shoulder. Without saying anything, he just stood there, consoling his dad. We had our difficulties over the years, but when it came down to the wire, my oldest son, whom I had abandoned years before, was there beside me. I'll never forget that moment.

There were no working phones anywhere, but somehow Dianne managed to get me a message that she would be flying into Fort Myers the next day and asked if I would pick her up. When I got to the airport, I tried to avoid her having to see the devastation as long as I could. We drove all around, surveying the damage of the town until I finally had to take her to her office. She was awestruck when we got there. As she walked around the grounds, there wasn't much to say other than my weak attempt to let her know things would be okay. A few of the guys had come in to offer whatever help they could, and there really was nothing we could do but start salvaging what was salvageable. There was about three feet of water in the remnants of each of the buildings, and all the records and paperwork were totally destroyed.

We always flew an American flag and a US Marine Corps flag outside of the main entrance, and we had taken them down when we knew there was a storm coming. They were somewhere inside of the building, scattered among the floating debris. As the guys and I were standing outside, trying to come up with a plan, Dianne suddenly came out of the building and we watched as she walked past us, saying, "I'm going to stick this somewhere."

She walked all the way to the front of the car lot, carrying the American flag. She looked around for a place to stick it and found a piece of chain-link fence that blew in from someplace and plunged the flagpole into the ground, using the fence to stabilize it. My God, it reminded me of the famous statue memorializing the US Marines' World War II battle at Iwo Jima. I looked at the guys and smiled. No victims in this family, I can assure you. We knew everything was going to be okay.

I had a business meeting with the entire team, about twenty-five people, within a day or two after the storm and assured all of our employees that we would do all we could to keep them working; we would understand, however, if they needed to make life changes because of the disaster. Giving them a place to work and stay busy seemed to be therapeutic for them because no one left; they were all anxious to get back to rebuilding. I was proud of our team, and they inspired me to come up with a plan to get things back on track quickly. How do you get back to business after a devastating storm destroys everything you have? It's really quite simple. You just keep moving piles of debris from one spot to another until it's your turn to have the dump trucks come by and get them.

For the first two weeks, we worked among the debris in our garage. I then purchased a small trailer to work out of, and we eventually worked our way up to two large trailers and a rebuilt garage. I had salvaged a few old three-part purchase orders, and Dianne had found the necessary paperwork to be legal, so even though there was no power, we would be able to sell cars if we had a customer or two.

People were going to need cars, that was for sure, but their insurance checks would be backlogged and payments would be slow in coming. We had excellent insurance, and within two weeks, the beleaguered agent arrived at our location, walked around every car or what was left of it, and shook his head. When he was done, he walked over and handed me a bank draft, which, of course, is money in the bank. I'll bet he didn't say ten words the entire two or three hours he was at our location. I looked at the draft and then looked at him and said, "What do you want me to do with all these cars now that you've paid me for them?"

He said, "Mister ... they're yours now, and I don't care what you do with them. I got ten thousand cars to appraise and get rid of. Some guy from Kansas will be coming around if you want to sell them to him." And off he went.

As fate would have it, three more hurricanes followed over the next six weeks. Frances, Ivan, and Jeanne each slowed down any recovery progress, and it was only after mid-September that we could get started on any rehab for our business.

The national media, of course, was all over this story. Water and food trailers were everywhere, and a realtor from Naples built a meal tent on their condo sales location in Punta Gorda. Somehow, it had miraculously been spared. When Dianne and I went there for a hot meal on day 2 after the storm, we were surprised to see my friend Al Speach, an old high school buddy. He was there with his wife, Terry, who had gone to school with Dianne. It felt good to have that connection at this challenging time. The Federal Emergency Management Agency (FEMA) was on the scene providing help when needed, and a virtual FEMA town of trailers was set up just outside of town.

There was talk of available unemployment dollars for those affected by the storm. Dianne and I both agreed we would not seek help. For some strange reason, the feeling of being a victim when we both were still capable of working was out of the question. Of course, there were many who needed the assistance, and we were grateful it was available for them. Ironically most of the local homeless were now housed in FEMA trailers and were living better than they had before the storm. But we wanted to keep our heads high and get to work.

The problem, of course, was it would be impossible to get any repair or bodywork done on the cars that were still saleable. All of the shops within fifteen miles had been destroyed as well. Somehow, we had to get the damaged inventory out of the way so we could get some fresh inventory. The totaled cars were moved to the back, waiting for the guy from Kansas, but we had a lot of damaged yet good running stuff sitting on the ground that was saleable. *Hmm*, I thought, *We need a plan.*

As I went into one of my trances a few days after the storm, it suddenly hit me. Most of the cars not totally destroyed still ran well, but they all had severe body, light, and window damage from flying debris and interior water damage from rain. I took out ads in surrounding town newspapers and radio spots advertising "The Mother of All Scratch and Dent Sales." The radio spot said something like this, "Come buy a car from Charlotte County's number-one independent car dealer, with a bit of hurricane damage for half price or less. Take it to your own body shop for the minor bodywork." It was amazing how many people we attracted who wanted to somehow be connected to the hurricane. I just couldn't understand it. I envisioned little old men sitting in their club saying, "Well, I got to go now ... Got to get my car to the body shop for hurricane damage," and their friends saying, "Wow ... were you in that hurricane?"

The sale was a tremendous success. We got a lot of National Automotive publication exposure primarily because we maintained a positive attitude and did not buy into the victim mentality. We all had our health. We were able to work, and we did. Our salespeople really loved the sale because they were now getting 20 to 30 percent from a cost of zero. In the end, the first full month back in business, after Hurricane Charley hit our town, turned out to be the best profit month in our company's history. And we now had cleared out our old stuff and were ready to make the rest of 2004 successful. We would just have to do it in trailers.

I thought about the old story of the difference between a pessimist and an optimist. It seemed to me that if you're willing to pray, work hard, and no matter what, head toward what seems to be the next right thing to do, somehow you can find a pony in what looks like a pile of horse manure.

It didn't take long for things to get rolling along pretty well. We would have to wait a while to rebuild, but with strong faith that showing up and doing the next right thing would direct us in the right direction, we had somehow adjusted and were doing as well in the trailers as we had been before Charley roared through.

We knew we were going to miss some of the deals from the old Gene Gorman Family location, since it was going to be impossible to rebuild there. After a year, we started looking for a new location in our neighboring town of Port Charlotte. Demographically, it was more of a blue-collar town than Punta Gorda and a lot of our BHPH business came from there before Gene Gorman Family Motors was leveled.

We came across a good spot and after some intense negotiating, opened our second location about two miles away from our original spot. We named it Gene Gorman Family Motors. It worked out perfectly.

There were a few obstacles we had to overcome before rebuilding Gene Gorman Auto Sales, and it looked like we might be in trailers for quite some time. The county had put new code and zoning requirements into any new buildings after the hurricane so it would be impossible to rebuild like we originally had things set up. Foreseeing a long delay, I decided to look for another spot in Punta Gorda.

There was a dealer down the road from us who had somehow escaped being totally destroyed and had done a nice job of renovating. As I drove by his place each day, I noticed his inventory was starting to shrink without being replaced. I knew he was either having a hard time making it or had just lost interest in the business, so I stopped by and figured I would plant a seed in his head. I said, "If you ever run across anyone who has a place like yours who might be interested in getting out of the business, be sure to let me know." Within two weeks, I received a call from him, and two weeks after that, we moved into his totally refurbished, like-new car lot. Since it was in the heart of the nicest section of town, we named it Gene Gorman Premier Auto Sales and started carrying an upscale type of inventory. We then called and had the trailers moved out. We now had two dealerships and two vacant lots.

Ironically, within another year, the county seemed to soften their stance on codes a bit, and we were able to build a brand-new building where our original site was. All we had to do now was decide what we were going to do with it. We decided to upgrade the inventory at our Gene Gorman Family Motors location and create another low-price car lot, since that demand was growing. These cars were often trade-ins from our other two locations. After debating with Dianne and Owen on what to call it, I decided to just flaunt the fact these were going to be our most inexpensive cars, and I chose Gene Gorman's Dirt Cheap Cars.

Since our slogan had always been "I'd give 'em away, but my wife won't let me," coupled with my picture on every sign, I offered Owen the chance to put his name and picture on the Dirt Cheap location. I'll never forget his comment. "So you want me to put my picture on the Dirt Cheap location? I'm out."

We laughed, and I agreed to put my mug on that sign as well. Our reputation in the community was our strongest attribute, so we figured why not take advantage of it with all of our locations?

# Chapter 17

## Getting into the Service Business

Ever since we had opened our first location, we had been paying outside mechanic shops to do all of our service work. Our sales outlets were not zoned to do service, so we contracted the work out. After the hurricane, our primary repair shop, which was right next to our original car lot, had decided not to rebuild and closed rather than renovate and buy all the high-tech computers necessary to fix modern-day vehicles.

Owen and I talked about the option of opening our own shop in his old place and buying all of the modern-day equipment, a very expensive proposition. He seemed more excited than I was about the prospect of getting into service so I assigned him the task of doing a marketing plan to see how long it would take to become a profitable enterprise.

A week later, he presented me with a most impressive marketing plan that accounted for servicing our own vehicles as well as going after all of the business that the old mechanic was doing for people around the local area. It was then that we decided to open our own service center in Punta Gorda, right next to what would become our Dirt Cheap location.

As fate would have it, we did the same thing in Port Charlotte when the Goodyear tire store was closing right next to our Gene Gorman Family Motors location. By 2008, we had three dealerships and two service centers, and business was booming.

I had come to the conclusion that except in a few rare situations, having a number of small businesses was better than having a big one. They are easier to manage and control, less costly, and much more profitable. My friends used to say I was the McDonald's hamburger restaurant of used-car dealers. French fries are the same at any McDonald's. Because of our systems, you were always handled the same way at any of our dealerships. This allows us to cross-sell and promote from within as our needs arise.

Pictures of some of our businesses

# Chapter 18

## We Won't Be Participating in the Recession

In 2008, the economy started its slide downhill. Many of our employees were nervous about the future because of all of the media buzz and the general "Woe is me" mentality circulating around the country. I assured all of our people that I had been through this stuff numerous times in the past and even mentioned a recession many years before, during the Carter administration, that by 1980 saw interest rates hit 22 percent with double-digit inflation. Most of them were not even born or were babies at that time and couldn't believe it. I then told them that we were not going to be participating in the recession; we were just going to work harder and smarter than we ever had before. I explained to them that my best year selling was in 1980 and most of the credit went to not buying into the negativity.

Average salespeople love to have excuses to be average, and recessions are a perfect excuse if you let them be. I clearly remember one of the salespeople at Checkered Flag coming in from hanging out at the door with the other average guys as I was sending out literature to customers. He said, "Hey, Gene, did you see the paper? Interest rates went up again to 22 percent. Can you believe it?"

I replied, "Of course I can. They were 21 percent yesterday."

His response was "What are we going to do?"

I said, "Well, I'm going to finish my mailing as soon as you quit trying to pump me up."

I then assured my team that we were on a level playing field with everyone else and we could really step it up, now that the underachievers were buying in to this recession stuff.

I had learned that negativity feeds on itself, and we were going to stay positive and not give negative energy the power to get us down. We had a few slow months, but after adjusting our attitudes as a company, we went on to enjoy a very successful year.

As I wrap up this seeming success story, I am sometimes still surprised at the power of maintaining a positive outlook and continuing to show up each day where I'm supposed to be and when I'm supposed to be there and not worrying about results.

# Chapter 19

## Civic Responsibilities—Giving Back

A big part of our community connection has been our signage. As part of our marketing plan, I felt having my picture on the sign as well as using my name gives potential customers peace of mind, particularly important when buying a used car.

I also felt I owed the community that educated my children and made us successful a lot. So in 2004, the year of Hurricane Charley, when the community was reeling from being destroyed, we started sponsoring tournaments for the local high school athletics. They have been running consistently for twelve years. Each year, we have been fortunate enough to sponsor a girls' volleyball invitational tournament as well as a boys' wrestling showcase. The top teams in the state are invited to show their talents to local college scouts and coaches, hopefully generating scholarships for top athletes. We also award a $1,000 scholarship to the athletic fund of the school in the name of the outstanding player/wrestler in each tournament. It has become a very big deal to these bright young student athletes as well as their schools' sometimes tight budgets. In addition, we donate five thousand dollars to the football program each year to show our support, and we are the main sponsor of the local Punta Gorda city golf championship, which features eight of our local high school boys and girls team members and generates thousands of dollars per year for the Juvenile Diabetes Research Foundation, or JDRF, as well as local community charities. It goes without saying that "giving back" has become Dianne's and my personal passion. We feel we have much to be grateful for, and we try to show that gratitude.

Not only do these activities present a positive image of our companies as good citizens, but they serve as a powerful message to our employees that they work for a company they can be proud of.

# Epilogue

As you have read, in the early days of my journey, many of the lessons I learned in my used-car sales career came from doing things wrong and making mistakes based on ego and not sound business principles. I have done my best to eliminate the things that are not useful and focused on only those principles that have worked for some of the most successful business owners and managers from around the country.

As I mentioned previously, one of my earliest nonautomotive clients was AT&T. After the deregulation of the phone industry, AT&T was no longer the only source in town, and they had to learn how to sell phone systems. I often chuckled, but it seemed reasonable to me that they would turn to a used-car dealer to learn how to sell. The principles of Action versus Reaction Management work in any industry.

I have tried to present my Action versus Reaction system of success message with real-life examples of what doing the next right thing each day will bring to anyone willing to hear the message.

While teaching our systems around the country, a couple of things become obvious.

1. Those who keep doing what they are doing will keep getting what they are getting.
2. It is easy for average to become the norm.

The law of success is a reality; often, the only thing missing is the belief that it will work for you.

The principles of Action versus Reaction Management can be easily adapted to any business. Search out what is necessary to create your own DAR and stick to it. Create one for each member of your team if you desire to become a leader in your industry. Establish your team's winning edge, and coach your team on a regular basis. All that is necessary is that you become committed and willing to stay committed to believing in the power of the law of success. The benefit of taking some time each morning to slow down before you get started can't be overstated. The messages will come to you as you go into your own little trance.

www.ingramcontent.com/pod-product-compliance
Lightning Source LLC
Chambersburg PA
CBHW032026170526
45157CB00002B/868